T0171186

Peace

of

Mine
Special Limited Edition

by
A Comeaux

authorHOUSE®

AuthorHouse™
1663 Liberty Drive
Bloomington, IN 47403
www.authorhouse.com
Phone: 1-800-839-8640

Photos by Darwin Comeaux for D. Comeaux photography on
location exclusively for A Comeaux in Minneapolis, MN atop
the Midtown Exchange building/The Chicago condominiums
rooftop. Hair and Wardrobe by A Comeaux

First published by AuthorHouse 03/09/2011

ISBN: 978-1-4567-3621-7 (sc)
ISBN: 978-1-4567-3620-0 (e-b)

www.MeauxWrites.com
A Comeaux
P.O. Box 7558 Minneapolis, MN 55407

Printed in the United States of America

A Paradox: Prose of Love and Lack thereof *original hand-
painted art designed exclusively for kd Comeaux by S. Lovell*

Ciara speaks courtesy of the most beautiful friendship known to
my life. Thank you, I love you, grateful to write with you.

This book is printed on acid-free paper.

To my Sun,
God's greatest extension of His love for me

Note to Reader from Writer:

I'd like to first thank you for delving into
my heart, thoughts and 1ˢᵗ effort to put
them together to make sense of it all!

But you must know a little about my writing style
so as to gain as much pleasure and comprehension
out of my work as I intend for you to obtain.
I use the word 'peace' as in piece because each
extension of my attempt to seek and reach peace
is in my work. Writing is my peace. It is the
peace that is me! And this collection is a collage
of my peace and sometimes lack thereof.
Go with me.

There are peaces in here that have little to no
punctuation. It's just how I write at times and felt
this approach fit the peace best. At these times, look
for Capital letters even in the middle of a sentence;
this will invoke a new thought or at least the break
up of the last sentence to assist in you pacing
yourself and keeping the rhythm of the peace.

Let's practice:
"She's wounded She's broken and bruised But
she's trying to recover from a love that turned to
abuse And it's no use Crying or to try to make it
work The song say love is sweet but no one ever
mentioned it hurt Now she's in pain and in her heart
there's such disdain So her soul bleeds tears of a
Lost Loves Rain…"

Hope this helps, otherwise log
on and ask me personally ☺
www.MeauxWrites.com

Table of Contents

Butafly Dove

A heart so young and passion filled-
To throb so sweet and softly killed.
A mind in a zone with a twilight thought-
They spin all around like a Butafly caught.
A body turned temple to a dome of love-
With a heart that beats mentally like a
Butafly Dove.

I Am A Writer
For You

Rev 1:19 Write the things which thou hast seen, and the things which are, and the things which shall be hereafter;

I write for fatherless children husbandless mothers and women misused I know what that feels like That burning in your heart that never quite feels right. I write for the wounded and broken in spirit Those beautiful souls silenced by pain and only kindred spirits hear it. I write for the lost where no place is home So like beautiful butaflies in the streets they roam. I write for daughters who look to they baby daddy for a father when he share that void too. I write for those looking for someone to love them Not realizing true love starts within You. I write for those who can't articulate their heartbreak but speak loudly with sexual actions Trying to fix an internal problem with an outside solution will never bring forth true satisfaction and it Shouldn't surprise you what a girl without self-love'll do for a little attention Taking looking for love in all the wrong places-to another dimension. I write for those who find solace in the bottom of orange bottles or in the arms of the same sex of another. I know. I know...And though, no I can't save you from any spirit that plagued you I know the God that delivered me is the same one that made You much more than brokenness could ever break you He'll retrieve you from wherever you let that life take you. I wrote this for those who had life sucked right out of 'em whether figuratively by them streets Money cars and bros or clinically through a hose Them ones who been told, 'I aint ready to be daddy!' quicker than you can put

on your clothes For ladies who had names picked out and
remember back like 'the baby would've been how old?'
I write because I know what it feels like to wanna jump
ship When you're drowned in emotional despair like
those slits really don't Scream you wanna call it quits but
Subliminally suggest your heart hurt so bad
you had to distract it with an outside fix
I don't write because I don't have nothing else to do. I
write 'cause I'm trying to get something to You. I write
to get loose those hung from a self-afflicted noose For
You who begging to hear your story out of somebody
else's mouth. I got you. I'm a writer and this is what I do.
For my son my rising Sun my 2nd shot at life It matters
not what I left but that I end up right You see I write
because I learned that pain pills don't heal heart ache,
and no matter how loud the holla There's nothing louder
than the shatter of a heartbreak, I'm writing for you.
With my pen's dukes up, in a verbal match of fisticuffs
I'm fighting for You. I write for those who been there
and those who went back Those who are there now and
have no knowledge of where they're at. I write because
pain has lead me to bottles I've drowned in But it was
in my High's low that my inner hope was found in So
I dig from there where they say the gut is and I choked
hurt abrogated confusion and killed self-hate for causing
all this emotional ruckus and I wrote my Sanity's Plea. I
write so vehemently due to the degree of love, joy, pain,
and praise within me. I Write like my life depends on it I
swear by my journal and college ruled blue lines because
my pens on it. I write like it's my prescription for a good
nights rest, my personal cheat sheet for life's unpredictable
test. I write because I have questions the average mind
can't reply like How can I be chosen to give Spiritual
birth when my inner demons tempt me daily to abort or

by A Comeaux

What happens to my innocent passions if I'm called
to teach and bring the Word forth... I'm a Writer and
I do this for Life It's like my mind had an extreme
makeover You can say my thoughts been under the
knife Like my fingers held my laptop hostage in a
talented hostile takeover My my words been over
taken by verbs I've never heard of in my life!
With juxtaposing views, past pain and present blues
Some take it out on themselves I take a vengeance with
penmanship You settle your life's differences however
you choose So I penned this peace for those in grief to
know what Peace looks like I used to be hell in heels
now this is what peace looks like. I wrote this to say
Don't fret and never stutter Be clear on your desires and
when you're weak you must utter up all your gumption
and might To believe that your worth it You're worthy
But you must 1st conceive these things relieve these
rings and free yourself from yourself You are your only
hurdle Get back tight with loving You like your mind
heart and emotions was wrapped snug in a girdle and
Just breathe and let go Any energy taking you to a place
your spirit cant grow A place where you cant be the best
you That's an avenue you can't afford to stroll So when
oppression pushes you and reveals what you been through
Don't buckle-Step up even if you feel hell is what
you been going through I wrote this to say though
we may never speak and our eyes may never greet
We share a passion a love a struggle a victory we are a
People I wrote this peace right Here because I need you
So when your spirits low and your hope is
teary eyed Let your pain cry and know
A Comeaux is writing for you

4

**They asked me who I write for. 'You' was my reply and if I'm wrong there's nothing better to be right for. I can tell you why run-a-ways stray and who fiends light for. Why the beaten wife stays and who the bullies fight for. Who dope boys cook for and what lesbos dyke for... Most times Love. Or lack of childhood hugs. So we grow accustomed to the weakness of who we believed in, creating our own demons and sanity-clad drugs with soaked pillows we've grieved in. Ever saw picture sans your face but you were supposed to be seen in? Thought you were in it when everyone else was. And regret has a grip on your absence like an ill-fitted glove. Perfect. In darkness one can't find light when they're spirits eyes closed and the depths of the broken soul the world will never know. I'm. One. Of... Them. Too. They judge my decisions as if I was putting them through! What my choices, desires fetishes and insecurities would soon ensue!! Oh my. I'm my life's truth and me words no lie. So, yes, I'm still writing for you.. And I...

Love,

A Comeaux

Your Color

"What color are you today little girl?" She replied, "Oh, today I'm a deep shade of blue. I have a crimson undertone due to what my mother is going through. But check with me later. My favorite shade is a much lighter hue. But we can't worry about that now, we've better things to do. See, some days, when he calls and says he'll be over soon, she's happy so I'm happier than when school lets out at noon! But two days it's been, feeling more like a week. That she didn't see him no we haven't seen him and he has not the decency to speak. So today, miss lady, I'm the color of a summertime midnight. Don't look so confused miss lady. You're thinking this is too much for a kid, right? Well I agree! But I mean, what can I do? Blue is a beautiful color, right? No matter what the hue." I walked away feeling heavy like melancholy like in sorrow. She ran up to me, almost out of breath and panted, "Don't forget to check with me tomorrow!" So I did and when I watched her, before me she didn't see. The shade in her eyes the deep shade of demise, was two times twice as deep. "Little girl, needless to say, the shade in your smile, the lack of a smile gave your mood away." But this time it was like a view, a view of Lake Michigan in the am of 2. Beautifully serene yet dark indeed. The hurt of a child from a mother's heartbreak is enough for us all to grieve. The weight of a heartache. The burden of loss. The fact that she feels the shade of the rejection no matter the cost. Undaunted.
And still tender in heart.
She loves whom she sees and bleeds when they part.
"He's gone for good miss lady, so what color are you?"

Dear Lord,

I'm sorry about you letting you down, like I knew you knew I'd fail but I feel like you also know I knew better I mean you Did give me a way out and I stayed there I stayed where you told me not to go in the first place I wanted to Felt I had to I mean you saw him You created him You knew what he would say Anything and everything for him to get his way And though he didn't touch me He took me My mind and heart that you've cleaned up and restored for your glory Well it's all focused on him and what he said and what he did and how he did it and how much he loves me and I love you really you know I do but I've got bigger issues than these whims of affection and what they put me through. Dear Lord, yes I'm single but I feel so attached to one or another and that's not the plan no that's not what you planned you said it's best to serve you alone And though no one is home there's always one in my phone One in my face One in my past and they take turns to replace One for the other in any given season. Dear Lord, please help these people to leave me be I seek to serve you in mind and heart with all sincerity But it's hard and yes I say no and truly mean it It's just that sometimes I tend to make messes in hopes that you'll forgive me and clean it so Dear Lord, this is my letter and I hope you do read My heart my little heart that so desperately needs...
You. Dear, Lord.

What Becomes of the Brokenhearted

So I ask what becomes of the brokenhearted
What happens when your soul and your mate is
parted What will become of the heart left to bleed and
grieve all alone in darkness where your joy can't see
How does one mend after the loss of their
hearts friend and try to fit in the healing
box but these ruff edges won't bend
Cause it hurts now
and pain is as strong as the pleasures of love
Agony in place of appreciation
meditating on things a sane heart would never conjure up
Like the picture of you without
Us
So what do you do when the love of
your life no longer loves You
Stop living?
A heart is meant to love receive hugs
How dare heartbreak ask me to stop giving
I'd rather be told to stop breathing
Cause right now I'm bleeding from
needing an arm to hold Me
I didn't listen to my mother when she told me
"Love don't love nobody"
Or maybe that was a song
But my heart tells me they're all wrong
Love taught me love
Like hate It's learned It's kept and given
It's the place when blushes from a
crush grow to being Smitten
By love

And I wish it would stop there where butaflies
flutter around where my unborn child is So
So I ask you what becomes of a woman like me
I want to love but I'm afraid
I'm willing to hold you baby be your fantasy lady but But
I have this broken heart in my hands and
my emotions said forget a roller coaster
They're dangling on sanity's strand
And
Well
I really need to know
What becomes of the brokenhearted
But here I am with blood-tear stained clothes
I'm drenched in a heartache that only my poetry knows
Cause my heart can't take the reality my fallacy shows
So I add myself to the list a million hearts want to know
How to fill the void of a love missed
How to get a peck on ones heart
How to get my emotions kissed
This rhetorical question I speak of but we all want to know
Where does ones heart end up when
there's no place for our love to go
What really becomes of the brokenhearted
A love left to roam w/no valid destination
due to a detour after we started
Like a road trip gone bad
I feel like a hopeless romantic gone mad
Like my love's used goods some fool done had

But I
I still believe in you
I know your power and the mere presence
of your existence resembles that of an
Ecliptic Sunshower

by A Comeaux

Pure Beauty
All I ask is that you return
But you live learn move on and grow
The whereabouts of the brokenhearted is one
we'll never know
A place we've all traveled
But never volunteered to go

Never Alone, Never Again
For NA

*I met you when I was 9 and it was something like
running into a long lost cousin at a funeral; Happy to
see them but misery pervades your optimism due to the
circumstance. So here I am with the 1ˢᵗ love of my life. My
best friend. And he has a problem. A problem that my
hugs can't heal. A problem that my kisses can't nurture.
And frankly I'm pissed. I'm pissed because my mom is at
work. Work! This is her husband, not mine. I'm a kid
for crying out loud! But he's mine. My Daddy. So I'm
here in this meeting and I see these grown people, these
adults, who've lost their way. Some are helpless. Some
are here for perfunctory satisfaction while for others this
is the last stop. I heard you. I'm here, so here's to you...*

You've given me a humility that only hard times and
brighter ones can appreciate. You're not alone. I walked
that dark street on that lonely road in that desolate city;
looking for my daddy. While the world turned daily
and new nights came with the same mares. I was lost
looking. With tears in my eyes and confusion in my
heart; I was looking for my daddy. Never again, he told
me. He wouldn't face me when he stared his addiction
in the face and shame is what kept him. Kept him from
calling or being called, 'daddy.' It was Father's Day and
special because it too, was my birthday. I thought that
was cute. Not you. Who didn't notice and I couldn't find
the only one I wanted for my birthday. My daddy. I was
19 and he was roaming like a cell phone with charges too

high to pick up and say, "Hi, bey! I love you and I'm ok."
Ok, he wasn't and when I finally found him it was here.
In these rooms in these meetings in this program that
says It can work if you work it. 30 in 30 and so on and
so forth. I had to share him with his addiction. With
those streets that stole so much from me. And today,
NA is where he finds his purpose to speak and be a
light A pillar in this community of father's brother's ex-
whores and convicts. A room full of men who may not
have an I.D. but have a desire to never use. Never use. A
room full of men who pray for those not as fortunate to
make it out. And into. NA. There's hope there. There's a
power of brotherly love and inspiration. You, NA, make
me grateful for each day I have clean. Though I never
stood up and professed, "I'm an addict named..." In life
we have to find our own way and peace and light and
God and help and I've found mine. In the God of My
understanding. But my daddy, he's a Powerful speaker
and it gives me chills thinking about it there's no doubt
I get it from him! He's the picture of a good thing gone
bad that got back right like never before. And he's never
alone. See I'm his babygirl, I can't talk about hear and
relate to that part of his peace, You NA can and I thank
you for being You for being there where my love could
never reach. I still go to meetings for ole time sake. I
remember you and how we first met. Like the 1st grade
teacher who seemed too hard on me on my first day and
all I wanted to do was color and play with my friends.
But I've grown to love you, NA. Like I still remember my
teacher's name in my gratitude. I love you for the man
that has come out of those rooms. I still make it to all of
his speaking engagements and he still gives me chills and
I still tear up when he tells the room, this room full of
addicts and those who keep at it, about my piggy bank.

About that night I begged him not to go, not because
of the money, I knew not the capacity of its weight. I
wanted my daddy to just go to sleep. Put it down and
go to sleep. Didn't grown-ups love to sleep, too? But he
left and I was mad pissed hurt and confused. I hated
that thing that made him do such a thing. And you,
NA, identified it and helped him talk. Talk and talk
and speak and share and Sponsor and share some more
and I think that's a pretty good deal. He's not alone,
not because I love him, but because he's found a group
of souls seeking clean living as hard as he did, and it's
worked. Here's to you! Men and women who shared your
secrets in hopes of getting free and hug as a greeting and
talk to much jive and get too loud and smoke too much
and who keep coming back. He's home. And though I'm
grown now I remember that little girl with that grown
man when I was strong and he revealed his weakness
and we were afraid together. There together. Still...

kco

Hi I'm kco. Flow like yayo. Addicted to my dictionary. I'm
Word. Play Pro! 'I'm coming soon'. The main attraction.
Say GO!
8 hunit dolla heels. Dress thrift store vintage.
Zebra prints on my thighs.
Gucci aviator lenses. My style straight crazy.
Yes, I do fashion sorta senseless.
Ooops, I'm a Writer and Google is my witness!

I scuttle over nonsense, the rebuttal to your recompense.
Moms schooled me to Webster and we been together ever
since! I get off giddy from wordplay, like the anticipation
of a Thursday. Here comes the weak end! I'm stronger than
your minds broke link, let a piece of my speech seep in.

"Here comes, kco!" build my vocab like Diego. So I can
stack chips un-delay, bro! 'So she can write and speak too?'
Ha! You silly naysayers, I use night vision to peep you.
Now watch me fly by on the wings of good
times… 'Are we having fun yet?'
Narly!!
But I'm not done yet. Nah, not hardly…

Ay wut tha heckster! Wuts tha mollywhoppin problem?
U silly flippin wastrel! Sit up. CRUNCH! Go Jogglin!
Neoligsm: wutchanot! kco wordplay lucid. Obtrusive
in ya face and you're just past tense stupid…

Moonlit Love

Its dark here This is my heart here
And I call you Love
Its deep there
Who can keep this there
Where all my passions are thought of...

But this is real here
You can feel here
Like you never did before

The sad part Like the bad part
Is that you want so much more

You'd give more than you did the last time
Remember? That last time you gave your all

That past time That was last time
when long hard and slow was the fall
So I ask this Thinking you should pass this
Chance at another heartbreak
I pose this And who knows this
Who knows the limits lacking love can take

How many kicks can a hoping heart handle
Before the ceiling of grief caves in
How many stumps does it take per month
Before the days out of love out weigh the days in?

It's dark here
This part here

by A Comeaux

The part where you and I first met
It was sweet here
So sweet where I remember vowing never to forget
It's a Moonlit love that lights my sky
No apples
Melancholy glaze adorns my eyes
Talk about a bed purchased too firm
A policy clearly states: No Return
Some R&B crooner ushered to let it burn
Let It Burn
And oh how we love to play with fire
Sacrificing our logic for a chance our desire...
Is fulfilled
But more so than not it's silently killed
Why Moonlight, Why darkness?
All for the thrill
The thrill
The Thrill. How does winning feel?
Glorious
Notorious
Failure that is
A threesome summoned Relentless
The eldest of their kids
We try again after a heartbreak After all a heart can take
And still tell moonlight
Blissful sunshine is usually fake
Moonlit love
All the light this dark place needs…

Dodgin' Raindrops

Your love is like memories that never happened
Like actions thoughts and verbs of an
encounter I still cant fathom
Sometimes you hurt me
An unseemly cold feeling
Cold drops on my face
I'm in your storm
It used to be warm here How'd we get in this place?
It used to be sweet here Like Summer showers on my face
Them raindrops you look up to Eyes closed Open Wiiiide
That kind of love that soothes you while it consumes
you w/consequences sublime-Reality dampers the
intention and asks, "What are you in the rain for if you're
afraid of getting wet?" Like, why make me remember
your love if my heartbreak you're inclined to forget?
And I
Just can't get around you
I'm drenched like overwhelmed by your love yet
I'm nowhere around you
Frozen teardrops of a once blazin' lava spot
And what this all boils down to is
I bless curse regret and fantasize on
the day that I found you
But I was lost
Then
God found me and I revisited that place
Again

At first you didn't recognize me and now I don't know you
It's amazing what changing seasons will show you

What curve balls in the game of love w/
lack of time will throw you
Like feeling indebted to who you borrowed
from when in actuality they owe You
But it's cool now
Like an August afternoon rain
Yeah, we've cooled down
And what I've found is you'll go 'round and 'round
No matter how long it takes you
To realize the reciprocity of love inevitably takes Two
You'll get it
How a whole lot of disappointment
inadvertently breaks you
Or how
Amidst your desires breakdown
Life's actually disclosing what makes
you. Whole. Complete.
Resilient to defeat

When I become my best love None other can compete…
But lovin' you?

Lovin' you is like Dodgin' Raindrops Like self
induced trauma while beggin' for the pain to stop…
Stop…STOP…stopstop…SSS…ttoppp...
Please

Ima Do

Ima do this for you and Ima do that
Ima do all this as a matter of fact
Ima have you smilin make you sho nuff happy girl
Ima have you clean stlyin nails did hair never nappy girl
Ima give you all I got as soon as I get on
Ima give you more sweet good love soon as I get home
Ima take care of you your mama and kids too
Ima man a real man and thats what I'm supposed to do
So Ima go now Ya know I got things to do
How else can I get and do all this for you
Ima cool type of cat that know how to handle his biz
But with all this going on Well the thing of it is
Ima bout to have to leave But I wont be gone long
Aww dont look like that suga pie Tell daddy whats wrong
Now I told you Ima do it Just as soon as I can
Now dont you go looking for no nother two timin man
Nawl baby not you
You know you all I got
But I got to lay low cause the block done got hot
But I gatchu For real Ima hookit up real nice
Ima even buy you a big house Ima make you my wife
Ima have the whole hood mad
They gone be mad at you for real
Ima do so much for you girl You think its unreal
Ima buy you TV's computers Even fur coats
Ima ice out your finger wrist and matching bling for your
throat You'll never have enough Ima give much mo'

Ima be your best friend and everything you desire
Ima be like your drug girl You've never been higher

by A Comeaux

Ima be there for ya for real
Ima be like 100 years old and in love with you still
Ima upgrade your mind and certify your understanding
Ima be cool with you girl not all demanding
But Ima need you to respect me and give me my space
Ima leave as I please so don't go gettin all in my face
Know your place and Ima keep you mine
Other wise Ima move around on you
And wont give you no time
Ima get a better job Ima get my license straight
Ima move out from my mom's crib and get my own
place Ima even get a car so I don't have to drive yours
But girl you be at work all day Why let the car sit for?
Ima mover and shaker
You know I need wheels to make my runs
Ima put the gas back Ima lotta things but I aint no bum!
Ima cool dude and you know it
That's why you love me, right? Ima take you
places, girl, places straight outta sight!
Ima hold you down Ima keep you around
Ima do me and never be found
Ima roller, girl. Ima bad man the baddest in town!
But ok I'm about to leave
Ima be back soon indeed
But while I'm away on this lil stay
This is what
Ima need…

The Paradox of Life

The song say, "Drive slow, homey" I been moving too fast and
quick thrills don't last Life's about who makes it Not about
who's making it fast So needless to say pain done snuck up on
me And on top they say it's lonely Its really not they just phony
and regardless of my bruised mind and confused heart They
still on me! I'm at a crossroads of what I left and doing right
Give in to deceiving sin or strengthen my spirit for this fight...
I know I know... and with each strike I grow I'm a survivor!
Even in pitch darkness I glow...

If you ever took a pain pill when the only
thing that hurt was your heart
or wound up at your wits end and can't
pinpoint your turmoil's start
Then
You'll get this
You'll feel these words as if your ears were fingertips
Touch congregated verbs with reminiscent mental clips
Cause
We've All 'Been there and done that'
But only a few true ones speak of when they went back
Like Air Jordan's circa '95 Retros
or that lie cheat and deceiving sweet nothing
that your heart can't seem to let go
Though promises made sweet love found hate and
you wished you would've saved 15% with that Gecko
It's just no guarantees
When your mind gets spent and your heart
gets broke there's no warrantees
You stuck

by A Comeaux

with a defected piece
Perpetuating infected grief--
That man stole my good sense like satan's
hand selected thief Sidebar:
Ragged loose ends never get tied and
tears shed from hearts wounds seldom get dried
It's the face of an idiot when you believe their truths only
to realize they lied
The Paradox of Life
It's learning what you've always knew
or mastered a thing you swore you'd never do
It's bleeding by love seeing life in blue
I'm here to say earnestly I've been there too
I've been where you can't see think or breathe
nothing but the air another blew!
I've been through...
The fire
Only to return again
Once used to abuse it gets easier the time after again
This 'want what you can't have'
got you chasing what you can't grab And
looking for longevity in flings-n-things that can't last
And you ask, "How can one thing be so true and yet
be not so?"
It's the paradox of holding on to the one
you love and letting yourself go
It's the familiarity of the future The mystery of the past
The equilibrium of unstable emotions
And time that never pass
It's yearning for the forbidden when
Heaven is what you desire
It's too extreme to fathom that the contrary
will lead to what's dubbed as eternal fire

And this is Life on the daily and as
months go by turned years
We notice what we left behind is what we wish
we could embrace in the present Like
Right here
in the Now but this is life on life terms
Even though you thought you penned the rules
Other than the written Decalogue
There's no guide to life and living
It's a series of choices and how you choose
Will determine if you're one to win
or those accustomed to loose
Those living for the thrill of success or
those familiar with the hangover of failures booze...
They say, "Live everyday like it's your last!
Carpe Diem and Plan for tomorrow."
I've learned these tidbits to collectively
be true at one time or another
The paradox appears and asks on any given day it can go
any given way-How's one to know one from the other?
Life's not about the validity of lies
It's about finding your purpose and
drawing your own truths
The paradigm by which you measure your
conclusions is exclusively up to you
Or is it
When some decisions are made for you
Married for money the kids or a Man that adores you
The Paradox of leaving a place you've never been to
While crying tears in your emotions
that your heart has never been through
Or when you may have showed up
But you just wasn't there

by A Comeaux

With a constant heartache on top of a
heartbreak and now you just don't care
The Paradox of begging for love
when it's not what you need
More like, Time alone
To face yourself and adequate space to grieve
Hurt people Hurt people
Therefore pain is translated
The Paradox of Life proves living will be lived
It's 24 to every 7 to 52 no matter how you take it!

Chica-go-rilla

That Skyline
The L
111th Street
Michigan Ave and The Gold Coast

This my city My windy cold city Every buddy from
school always wanted to come home with me to see

Sock, candy and towel sellers on 95th St.
Maxwell Polishes
115th Street Beauty Supply and Air 1's
Downtown and Buckingham Fountain

This my city My cruel cold city every time I left everything
I took my baggage with me and I came back to see

Ruth's Chris and Shaw's
The Donut Shop in Roseland
Rush St.
The Boutiques on Oak St.

This city I keep leaving but can never stay away from
It came from me living in the 'burbs so the city always
been a treat to me and it beats me why I can never stay
But I'm a Chica-go-rilla no matter where I lay...

Papadeaux's
The Taste of Chicago on Fourth of July
Metra Transit
Foot work

by A Comeaux

This city taught me how to dance and move my feet faster
than Twista rhymes This city My city taught me how
Step before the name of love made it to the big times

The Garden's
63rd St.
The Lake Front and Lake Shore Drive
Navy Pier

This city birthed some of the most influential never
before never again pillars and they stayed here
Talk shows and played here This city is My city no
matter where I go this city is always with Me

Chicago Style...
Caramel Corn & Cheese Popcorn
Andy's Hair Studio
Jordan's

This my city I'm born and raised here in
this wind so know it's just a matter of time
before I breeze through again...

Life Support

It's the pain that keeps me alive. Well, it makes me to know that I'm living. That I'm not dead like how I feel on the inside. Cold. Detached and unaffected. Lifeless but reminiscent. I used to feel something like peace. Like happiness on the inside that got me through tough times. Something like one would call a reserve. A tank of goodness to pull from when you were out; and somehow it was replenished effortlessly. There when you need it most. Most of the time I was ok. But my reserve ran out. And that replenishing source evades me. No association. Nothing to do with me. That's what love does when he leaves. And if I'm not good enough for you to love me, after all I've given, then how can I love myself knowing that my best failed. So yeah, the pain keeps me alive. My fine line of hope and depression. Pills are too close to acceptance. Like a criminal taking his crime to the grave, this is a pain I won't confess to. Wont surrender to. Won't succumb to. Victim to? Yes. But my pain dually reminds me that I'm alive. At least I can cry when it hurts too bad to speak. At least I can grieve and let my inner spoil reek. At least I can bleed if the blade do me justice. If the knife serves me right. At least I can war with my inner darkness in the privacy of my nights. Ever left home running, so far you passed where you ran to, roaming through life juggling what pain hands you? If home is where the heart is, and mine was broken before I knew it, then did I ever have a fair shot before someone, somewhere blew it? Pull the plug. I'm ready to live!

When Best Friends Become Mothers & Mothers Become Best Friends

When mothers become best friends, a bond in the making is revealed. Finally, I understand her. Her expectations, her fears. Her joys of watching me grow into my own person. A woman. A mother. Who else could understand and help us other than the magnificent ones from which we were born. Our mothers. Through our differences, strong wills and contrasting similarities, my mother became my best friend the day I found out I too was called to the greatest duty a woman can be appointed. Mother. Care giver. Teacher. Nurturer. Disciplinarian. Role Model... Today and for all those to follow for the rest of our lives; we'll share and learn 'mothers wit' and be bonded by the circle of life forevermore... When best friends become mothers; for us it meant yet another journey we'll embark on together. Some 20+ years ago I met you, and your very pregnant and beautiful mother;. Me being the smallest 2nd grader in our class, I remember thinking, " She's the most prettiest super tall person I've ever seen, and her daughter's pretty nice too!" And from then on we shared picture days with missing front teeth, limo rides to Mickey D's (thanks Dennis), our 1st boyfriends, heartbreak AND revenge!! Freshman year in Arbor Trails complete with one stolen Lexus which was later returned and a New Year's Eve no one will ever forget! Fast forward two years and a few bra sizes to the infamous Bout It clique!! Oh MY!! We've been there and seen ALL that in our travels around the U.S. But Nothing prepared us for this next Adventure into Mommyhood! We've swapped many a story over the phone while states apart, But NOTHING tops the one where you say, "I'm pregnant!" and I scream, "ME TOO!" I'm delighted to share this pinnacle of my life with such an awesome best friend and 'play cousin'. May God keep you and your precious baby boy along with your new family and all things you put your hands to. Be Blessed and know that I look forward to another chapter in our lives together as Best Friends Become Mothers

Gemini

Hi, I'm One. And I am The Other. Good afternoon,
I'm the Sun and this is the Moon. We pass one
another frequently, oftentimes too soon.
See she is the life of the party and I, well
I'm a bit subdued. I'm polite cordial while
she displays the Diva attitude.
See we live together. Going on, well, plenty years now.
You'd think we'd get along nicely, at least you'd
think, by now. But there are times when I'd like
to sit and read, maybe people-watch or relax.
And here she comes with this grand idea. To
shop, flaunt, or move away and not pack!!
Oh my, this girl at times, drives me nothing short of crazy.
But the catch to this 22 is, we're wrapped in the same lady.
While I seek to please the Lord in actions and thought;
be a good girl and stay out of the way. She, on the other
hand wants to do her thing, flowing however she may.
I would love to be married with equal kids to pets to cars.
I'd like to take a vacation with the kids and one that's just
all ours. She's cool with the one she has and says, 'You
can't take a tribe to Italy!' She wants a high-rise condo
overlooking a skyline with endless water with equal cars
to careers to vacation homes in the sun. She wants a
man who loves her for life, even if that man is her son!
But me? I'm waiting on God. While she's still playing
the field. I know this sounds impossible, how can this
be true, too unreal! I know. I know. At least you get to
read about it, It's my Life! How do you think I feel??!!
I'm always torn, she's always pulling me and we war like
Spirit and flesh. But we love each other. We are each other.

We're one to describe it best.
She's a good girl, indeed, and even I have a wild streak, so
I guess it balances out. But there'll come a day when we
both can play and then we can really Rock Out!! She likes
a goon, a certified street-cred havin' no-nonsense dude.
A Soldier, them ones outlined in that song.
Me? Give me a geek who's sweet, loves to read and recite
poetry... now how can choosing a man ever go wrong??
It's crazy! It's a battle we fight on the daily. I want him,
she let another in and No one is fully satisfied. I guess you
can say take turns, ya know, kinda like a roller coaster
ride. These sides, these people, seem so much at times.
Who do I blame? What do I do? I embrace the true
Gem In I...

Because You Loved Me
For Abba, Father

I won't let them touch me anymore I keep my clothes
on and my eyes open Because you love me. I won't let
them make me into one that you didn't create me for or
degrade me for. I'm your woman. Your daughter. Yours
in mind, heart and body. Because you love me. I love
me. Because you kept me I now know I'm safe in your
embrace. Because you love me. You won't let me fall. I slip
and sit in the lap of my emotions. But gently you lead me
back to you and I know it's because you love me. I know
who I am because you love me. No one can tell me I'm a
freak. A dyke. A whore. An addict. A lost soul, nope! You
love me. Me! Who used to do that and them too? Yes.
The one who ran with that crowd and tried this and that
too? Yes! Me? How? With these tattoos and piercings?
These memories and them ones remember me too? Me?
Yes! You loved me in the depth of my transgression.
You came for me in the pits of my depression
At the height of my confusion...And saved me!
It meant so much more the second time around. All the
new wrongs on top of broken rights, You loved me.
You cleaned me up and wouldn't let that life, that
dark lonely life, have me. I know them. I used to
be them. They're still there. Here I am! Because
you loved me you extended your arms and gave me
the purest affection my body has ever experienced.
Dana-Jahziah. My God, how you love me. When I
planned to leave, all along I heard your whisper but
you spoke to me so loudly Because you love me. I
can cry at the drop of this thought. You Love Me!!

That liar. A cursing, smart-mouth girl? Yes! You Loved me and my life shows it. I can feel it. In my loneliness I know it's your will. In my solitude it's you who keeps me company and I'm satisfied. I'm completely whole with your love. Lacking nothing. Because you love me, I can love now. I can breathe and release now all those things that had me bound. I'm Free because you love me. In my weakness you remind me of who I am. Yours. For a purpose. For a word that will not return to you void. I'll go, Father. I'll do it. Because you love me the world can't scare me into an addiction or trick me into affliction... anymore. You love me, now. Now I see this has been there all along. I am yours. I belong to a loving and tender, correcting yet merciful God. Because you love me I can go out in the world and not look for approval in anything but You. Because you love me. I can tell them No and not care who tells them Yes. YOU love me. And if he wants me he'll have to ask You for me! Because you love me I know what real love is and no man, no sex, no money, no 'thing', no trick, no trap, no one can take this away from me...Because you love me, he'll have to love You...

Woman w/Child
For Big K

She was young and in love oh how smitten
she was Motherless nonetheless
How beautifully graceful she was
A smile that can warm a room
Quicker than ice cream melting in summer's noon
She was delightful indeed
Look ahead
Now she's wed to the man of her dreams
Her virgin love Her 1st love The plan of her dreams
They had a baby A baby girl though he was told 'it's a boy'
She was pleased Elated indeed Her personal babydolltoy
Then he left He went away With the baby she was alone
No daddy for the baby No mama of her own
Who can she cry to Who can dry her rain
Her daddy was there Grandaddy was there
To love away her pain So she pursued her
dreams Her goals Her life She worked Went
to school and yet to become a wife
She traveled with the world on her on shoulders
Confusion in her mind
Years went by They both got older and
this is what they'd find
Not easy Never easy being alone in a
plan that somehow went astray
Never the plan No not the plan To go each's separate way
But she did it Did a great job I myself have to say
A woman w/child
Not just for her But for this child She had a way to pave...
Ran from there I was running from fear

Fear of success and of myself Made me run from here
Where home is
I wanted a love of my own
Reckless sex
Restless at best
God saw more than I could ever attest
Now she's pregnant Oh my Her? Pregnant?
How selfish The unselfish duty of this call
Does she have the endurance
The fight The wings for this fall?
She stayed He ran
More mind boggling than broken
promises could understand
She can take it Surely make it Will carry out the plan
Things will happen Things will fail
Things will be trying Things will prevail
God will keep her and teach that child
God will speak to and get through to that child
Like her mother She's a mother that
for hers will walk a mile
She's glowing I wonder why And knowing all the while
She's glowing cause He shined on her
Woman w/child
So with this new world on her shoulders
A baby on her hip
A promise to succeed
A vow to never quit
Woman w/child
She's the child of a Woman w/child
Child now a Woman w/child

Learned Practice

To fight to
Lie to
Cheat and to Steal

These things these wicked things
Are never learned from books no
Not read or told out loud, 'How'
But these things were done first then again
Then some more times before the victim learned
How...

To
Hate how to
Kill how
To rebel how to
Curse how
To rage how to anger

We watch mimic and learn things we never wanted to
before but somehow yearn things that someone had before

We do what is done to us even if it's painfully acted
We're mirrors of another's life in someway It's

Learned
Practice

To love and
To give how

To pray and respectfully
Live
To listen and to guide
How to mentor
How to strive how
To try and try again how
To play for sport how
To play to win

These things these golden things are in life like a token
It's amazing so truly amazing what
you can get with these tokens
But they must be taught They must be witnessed even if
not at home
They must be given They must be shown They
must be displayed They must be owned
Yes Practiced means done over and again Like always
These things are Learned they are observed
and that means attention must be paid

To write and to read
How to walk and run too
How to play and receive
How to start and to end how
To get and be a friend is all
Learned Practice

Tired/Tried

I'm tired of watching my phone like for missed calls
and unread text Like I'm tired of dudes thinking
'cause I already have a baby I'm ready and open for sex
Like I'm tired of being single Like I'm tired of aimless
relationships Like I'm tired of deceitful friends that wish
to have more than friendships Like I'm tired of church
folks backstabbing one another when we're taught to
With love cover our brother Like I'm tired of trying a
bunch of the wrong ways Like I'm tired of short nights
crazy dreams and long days I'm tired of watching and
feeling like I'm not doing enough I'm tired of feeling
overwhelmed 'cause I do everything alone and it gets
to all be too much I'm tired of my son's father using
my strength as his scapegoat--- That's so tired...

But it's all in the way you look at things like I've tried
to ignore warning signs but reaped the consequences
of what neglect inevitably brings I've tried to evade
that which must be confronted dealt with and only at
this point can one move on I've tried to end a thing
that somehow my heart allows to linger on I've tried to
fill voids that only God can supply I've tried hobbies
drugs men chicks hate self-destruction and found next
to salvation my only meditation is when I write...
They say try again if at 1st...
Being sick and tired of being sick and tired...
That's so tired! Get up and Try!

Random

I walk like I'm thick
Talk like I'm rich
Attitude match my shoes
Stiletto sharp wit
Expensive taste
Envied waist
A Comeaux birthed A L.O.M.O.
Abstract path I pave
Daddy got screeners
Mama keep new Beemers
Baby Ima cold piece of lava
Ex askin', 'Have u seen her?'
UPGRADE
Vocab equals hood made a baby with
Dictionary.com
Eloquent in speech Arch nemesis to defeat
Camarilla leader with on the spot charm
Do pardon my ostentation
Take a breath and relish in my poetic meditation
This prophetic medication is the cure for
Acrid salutation
Greet me sweetly or face a pugnacious situation!
You irritate me worse than the spot on wet socks.
I'm. What. That is. You're what that's not.
I don't write for free boo, I write to free you.
Priceless.

Miss de Marq

Here is my ode to you
The depths in lack of love I'd go thru…
Missing the Marq.
So young and naïve never recovered
from watching you leave
Cursed every ounce of man for redemption I conceive.
I simply didn't know better. Your love was the best
thing Ever. I simply didn't want to know better.
And years passed me and seasons too. Living a life
unfamiliar but made it all I knew. Simply because no
other man was you. You were like a star to me. But
I was living in darkness. Reaching for you in my ill
ways, so far I strayed, so far you were from me…
My heart, soul nor body could ever forget you. Pride?
Distance? My life simply wouldn't let you…
Come back.
Until you did! I was numb then. 11 years later.
Looking back, I thought I was dumb then!
But your rapture consumed me. Again.
With all I know I still let your tactics school me. Your
baritone from miles away fool me. Your web of deceit still
spool me. Like a shot in the dark in the core of my heart.
You owned my body leaving my conscience drooling…
To understand what I will never know. Loving a place I
will never go. Holding on to a dream when life says, Go!
So our reunion was simply closure. Giving my next
decade wings because this one, your era, is over.

Runnin' Shoes

For as long as I can remember
well maybe just a few years back,
no wait let me be honest
it's been about 10+ years as a matter of fact...
That I started runnin'.

He was a pretty boy a preppy boy lived further than me
in 'burbs. He wore sweaters and slacks to class and had
magnetic charm for the girls. But we were friends like
buddies and that was so cool at first. Had I known after
the truths wind blown I would endure so much hurt...

Go with me, I'll tell you how I got my
Runnin' Shoes

Louisiana. Michigan. Atlanta. Minnesota. Sprinkle
Chicago in there for good measure and this is what I do...
When I fall in or out of love.
Love and lack thereof...
I run...

Like I bounce like I never been there before. I walked out
on school and beat down Hard Knock Life's door and
they asked me, 'baby why? What are ya runnin' for?
You're so talented and attractive, Don't you want
anything more, than runnin' and startin over?'

My reply. Nothing drastic Just Manic and simply
didn't want to be here any more. In O.C. I
alienated myself for a girl and felt like it was over,

innocent years ruined. Not thinking Not clearly
thinking and had no idea of what I was doing...

When I got here and after I left there I still took
Me with Me and Oh what a shock that was. I
made the mistake of not addressing Self, what a
mental heart aching block that was. Atlanta. Oh
dear the trouble I'd see. But I was blinded. Self-
afflicted blindness and the perpetrator was me.

See I packed up three times. By this time. And even You
didn't notice I was gone. Mind Blown. Thinking anything
goes cause I'm grown. Oh my oh my had I known...

So I moved. Yep, packed my bags
and left everything I had.
No memories. No remains of a good heart gone
bad And the last one to witness is one I can't
call. A friend. Not enemies but it's best there's no
communication at all. And Oh when I yet again
moved I knew not the depth of my fall...

These shoes these faithful shoes Loyal only
to run. But they sang the blues The Blues
of my life is the only tune they sung.
But I changed them Yes I've changed and now I
sit and watch seasons pass. I wont wear them dare
not wear them Knowing this too shall pass.
I ran from disaster only to create chaos
and pain. This I know I surely know I'll
never run again. Stand up. Man Up.
Face 'whatever', eye to eye. I wont waste my time
running and watching life pass me by. A seed to
nourish a life to flourish is my chief reason why...

I left Chicago cause he hurt me and I didn't want to see his face. Ran to Louisiana only to feel morbidly out of place. Michigan was the next stop. And there I found true friends, until my fallacy got the best of me and then I went running yet, again. Atlanta hear I come! With pain in my eyes and a confusion riddled heart. One demon after another and I knew not my downwards start.

Oh the wounds. The scars. The tattoos. The mental bars. The Schools I enrolled in. But classes never taken. The things I tended to cherish only to find I was sadly mistaken. You must love You first!

I never understood that Like really comprehended. That if by fault a thing is started, there's a good chance that's how it ended. I turned on those who loved me and instead my enemies I befriended. I sold my joy for temporary gain and medicated a heart that simply needed to be mended.

Runnin' Shoes My runnin shoes. Riddled by fake love and up beat blues. My runnin shoes got too small. They wore out. I gave up. I kept pulling on the laces and tried to fix broken places but no matter what I did, they simply wouldn't stay up.

Bye bye runnin shoes. Thanx for bring me this far. Bringing me this far along. No blues, not in these shoes, I no longer hum that song.

But for those of you I passed and made acquaintance along the way Know that you're in my heart in a most sincere way.

Latifah, I still miss you and will continue to search, Jae
how are ya? Yes, I'm still, "too much!" Amber I hope
you're good and your seed is doing well, girl we have
some memories folks wouldn't believe but I'll never tell.
Marquis, I never touched him. He's your blood but he
lied. Envy is a poison that devours souls alive. This was
the heartbreak that ignited the turn of my life. But I
forgive you and wish the best for you but I'm sure you're
alright. If I ever see you, if again our hearts cross, I'd
hold your love for dear life. And give my all at any cost.
There are those of you I may see again, but most of you I
won't. I'll never forget you No never forget you and my
prayer is that you don't. Your friendships and kinships are
embedded in my mind. From Louisiana to Minnesota
I've found beings that are most certainly one of a kind!
Miss Debra from Red's trap, Solo from the club, lil
country from Southern U, thanks for showing me so
much love. Dorian from Blare, Verbert from Shipherd
and Shannon from Dole, Good bad and indifferent, in
the story of my life you respectively played a role. CTPK,
well, I'll see you all in a minute. This is for those I may
not, but it's for honorable mention. Most Adored, I hope
you're well. I hope your life turns out fine. That life is your
life and though for you I tried, it could never be mine...
The father of my Sun, man I tried to figure why. But the
truth is in all honestly, we were both living a lie. You
didn't know the hell from which I came and I couldn't
have imagined your picture was so broken with no frame.
No rules, no guides, no boundaries no lines. I never
considered an Us after our child you jeopardized. It was
too soon to love you, too soon to conceive, too late to
come back after you forced my soul to grieve. I cried in
the hospital, with wounds deeper than my flesh. I knew

I'd never trust you again, no matter the spiritual test. I knew I'd be alone. With a child on my own. And things only got worse as your past wounds were inevitably shown. You are God's child, and all His to fix. I couldn't mend your broken heart and knew I deserved better than this. Its been years now, seasons and holidays have passed by. Though I understand your distance, its our son who asks why. I tell him you love him. And that's all I can say. Too much for him to digest that his dad ran away. See my running shoes have taken me places that I never thought I'd see. At times turning me into someone I never thought I'd be. Saved and sanctified to a runner of the streets. Only by his mercy. And even after all these years, I still get the itch to run. In all truth I have but never at the sacrifice of my Sun. No matter the outcome, God knew what I needed. He gave me a sign and it was then that I heeded. He gave me the greatest extension of his love for me. No matter what I made of my body, He made a vessel for life of me. Wow. Will I ever put on my running shoes? I can't say no. but surely, oh, surely, I'll have my Sun in tow...

My Version of a Love Poem

...I know what falling in love feels like
Like I'm floating around cloud 9 on a kite
Like getting paid with no bills to pay
Its unreal how good loving you feels
I call your kisses aloe & cocoa butter b/c by
them my hearts wounds are now healed
And in life there's low places and long faces
and times hard side
But as long as you're there where my smile
can reside When my wings can't take off
your words offer my spirit a ride
When I shed tears the salty substance
provides a moisture to your lips and somehow
someway it don't feel so bad anymore
I'm in love
And the twinkle in my smile is how the world knows
'Cause my stride
It's something like a skip It's similar to a float
It's crazy each day how much my love for you grow
See I wear no make-up When I wake
up I'm dressed in a Lovers glow
Because I went to bed with
You in mind And like my heart
Loving you takes up most of my time
But before I brush a tooth I thank my Guardian Angel
for blessing me with You
You ole lovinmegently softlykissinme Tenda Roni
You
I could just bite you

If I could be anyone when I return
I'd pray to be just like You
My eyes are closed and in my palm rests my heart
I trust you as your companion I vow to do my part in
Loving you Holding you and Assure you
when you the world poses doubt
Like Air Water and Sunshine
Your love is an element I cannot survive without
It's us baby
We're like a chosen pair
Like where you are my scent is there
Like when you smile on the job and
no one uttered a word Like
hearing me whisper your name in the lullaby's of a bird
You're in love
And it's contagious
We were bit at the same time
Like one arrow from cupid we're so close
we were hit at the same time
How can we be so synchronized as one
I inhale
You release
I take one step toward you then our eyes meet
Who would've known the only air you'd breathe
is the air I blown And you still watch me at night
As I rest you still silently find refuge in the comfort
of my breast At ease My love Please My Love
Know this is your dreams home
Your crown is on your pillow and
together we'll share this throne
Know that if you went blind I'd give you my right
eye 'cause I can't see my life without you
You have 4 legs to stand on

If you ever get weary and feel you can longer
stand strong You can lean to me
Watching you Learning from you
When you need me I'll do what you would do
And together we'll win
Not only my love But my life's best friend
I can close my eyes and see your smile
I'd walk a mile for this love If I inhale deep enough
I can smell this love
It's Just That Sweet
How can you remember a thing you've never knew or
forget the worst thing you've ever been through
The same way I don't know
But will never forget
You
I am your wife and you are the best love of my life
If I had to have 4 broken hearts before I got to you
For this love Right here I'd gladly do it twice
I still get butaflies when you call I still feel the
drop in my belly as I relax and feel myself
Fall
Fall deeper in love In love I'm in love in Love
I'm in love w/the thought of being in love
And making these words come true
is all my heart dreams of...

A L.O.M.O.
For 329

A Mother's Prayer

May the Lord Bless your life. May He Bless your mind with peace and focus. I decree your mind be free from stagnation, confusion, and discouragement. I decree an honest and humble heart for you. Free from evil intentions and deceit. I decree your hands be Blessed with creativity; to build and not destroy. May He Bless your feet with divine direction and order your steps in His word to lead you into His will for your life. I decree Health and a strong body for long life. D-J, may the Lord God Bless all things you put your hands to for the Glory to His Kingdom. May you always have a friend in Jesus. May you always trust God and keep Him 1st in all things you do. I decree you to be a curse breaker, I decree you are head and not the tail, I decree prosperity and abundance over your life, I decree you to be a man after God's own heart. I decree your life is a legacy for generations to follow. I decree a focused mind, confidence in God when your world is filled with doubt. I decree you to be a secure and poised man. Responsible, and valiant, I decree your ways please God all the days of your life and He Blesses you with much mercy when if and ever you go astray. The word is in you and I trust God to raise you up in His Kingdom. Groom you for His purpose. I pray that if ever evil pervades your intentions and the enemy raises up against you, that you remember you are a child of the most high God. I pray you keep God first so you will be second to none. I pray your relationship with God is the one that you seek moreso than any other union in your life. It is your life line, Sun. Keep your Spirit alive. My Prayer, for my Sun.

A Mother's Promise

I promise to introduce you the Greatest Spirit in Life;
God. I promise to love you unconditionally. I promise
you a life of stability and sound direction. I promise
you an exceptional education. I promise to teach you
honesty and the power of your word. I promise to be
an example of what a Woman of God should be with
class, sophistication, intelligence, integrity, substance,
and direction. I promise to take you out of the country,
state, and home to explore and experience the world as
often as possible. I promise to never put a man before
you. I promise to nurture you and support you in your
talents and interests. I promise to be honest with you
about life and love. While I can't teach you how to
be a man, I promise to teach how to be a gentleman,
responsible and a man of integrity. I promise to allow
you to lead and use your best judgment. I promise to
teach you well enough to make your own decisions,
support you when you do and I don't agree. I promise to
let you grow into your own as a young man; into a man
who's wishes and choices I will respect because I know
what I've put in you with confidence in who God has
ordained you to be. I promise to listen to you. Always. I
promise to respect you. I promise to be nice to who you
bring home, Be careful baby, of who you bring home.
I promise you a good life. I promise to be your rock.
I promise to have a home you can always come
back to. In the mean time, I promise to have the
home all of your friends want to hang out at.
You are my clean slate, Dana-Jahziah,
I promise to never taint you.

A Mother's Wish

I wish you a full and meaningful life. I wish you love
and happiness in a woman who deserves you. I wish
you great friends, mentors, and inspirations. I wish you
favor in things you set out to accomplish for the good.
I wish you a book full of memories, and a lifetime of
pictures of your experiences. I wish you all the comfort
your heart can hold for your 1st heartbreak. I wish
you peace when disappointment arises, confidence
when rejection is present. I wish you direction when
you've lost your way. I wish you a friend in Jesus.
I pray God gives me the wisdom to understand that
you'll see pain that I may never know. I promise to hug
you when you need it most and kiss you in hopes of
removing hurt you didn't show. I'll give you confidence
and assurance when we both have doubt but all trust
in God. My wish is that I have the ability to love you
too much and yet let you go, live, learn, and gain your
own experiences life has to offer you. I wish you more
laughter than your smile can handle and more joy than
your heart can hold. I wish you a childhood that you
will be forever proud of. I wish you contentment in
heart and a sound mind. This isn't a wish, but I hope I
mean I really hope you're not embarrassed by me when
I'm always at your school, games, friends house to pick
you up and drop you off and basically show up any
given day for any given reason! My wish is that this
will make you happy and that you feel loved and cared
for. I promised you a good life. I pray God continues
to Bless me to give you one. And I wish you get it!
A L-O-M-O

It's Your Turn
For Me

Only in poetry can I say these things And only in prayer
will I heal these rings My powerful Kings and Queens
It seems we've lost our focus on the illusion of Bling
It's like we've been down too long been frowned upon
too long Ladies being laid with but left with sour
emotions too strong Woman you are worth far more
than what the media sells and Our children only know
half the story because we leave it to videos to tell

It's Your Turn

to be all things they said you couldn't be But that one
to surpass even what your imagination can't see Know
yourself and let no man define you Pursue your hearts
desires and cease things that bind you It's a big world
out there Break down the walls and free yourself from
history's chains Forgive those who broke your heart and
from your life remove their remains And when it rains
and even pours on days the sun was promised just know
As sure as yesterday passed better days will surely show
It is then your inner light will luminously glow
And no matter what you into or what you been through
You're beautiful Chosen to live a life that's Spiritually
dutiful You're better than what your sin was and
stronger than what gin does cause Everything in
motion shouldn't move you Be mindful of substances
that deceive to soothe you Cause in the midst of
the world wind girlfriend You'll loose you
With pain held in then your body cries out With so
many lies in you can't help but spit them back out And

53

you wonder where your love went With emotionless
relations and routine sedations Now you curious where
your hugs went Still low after yet another dub spent

It's Your Turn

to claim what the Creature ordained To take back
our history and it's stolen remains It's no mystery
We are bred from a people who once reigned

It's Your Turn

to stand strong though the walk is long we will never sit
in sorrow again Yes there's hate around us but we must
1st look from within This isn't slavery we're not made
to be mentally manipulated But spiritually extricated
praised and celebrated God does but Queen 1st and
foremost Love yourself enough to not stay stagnated and
conflicted Instead of going against every flow Just try
to go with it You can do all things through Christ who
strengthens you Why stay anyway thinking he'll change
too All that would do Queen is change you and All you
ever wanted was someone to hold you God created you
in His image How can satan mold you See I know these
things Look closely I still bare these rings on the surface
But now my inner love is protected where no one can
hurt it It's lonely but it's worth it I know that if I live
right I'll live peaceful I want more for my soul than them
cold streets do and I know the pain that loss cause
The strains of withdrawal and the pangs of loves fall
With these tattoos of mirrored malice taboos with
memories of a fallacy in the back of my mind asking me
Who's who! I feel what you going through But if you
feed your spirit and mortify your flesh Treat your body

as a temple then your mind will rest too And be careful who you look to What you see will be in you When your eyes tell what you've been through What will the mirror see I know what that life can do to you thought I been there and done that But it did Me when you're thinking you're the getter Better know you're still gotten How can you harvest fruit when your soil is rotten Maybe that went over your head How can you sleep in peace when your life's chaos rests in your bed What happened to morals once deeply rooted But with society so polluted it's not wonder our hope is diluted Like there's a target for destruction and guess what Queen You It See we must move on past that You must 1st visualize then go out and grab that life you know you deserve Listen to that voice God sent take heed and show Him you heard Seek ye first the kingdom of God and His righteousness and all these things shall be added unto you Queen God loved you 1st before and after what they done to you

It's Your Turn

to break these cycles we keep spinning in If not these rings and confusing things will be the pool of turmoil our minds'll keep swimming in

It's Your Turn

We're better on our feet than on our backs and conquering our defeat and making up for what we lack is a notion we must 1st attack

It's Our Turn

by A Comeaux

You're my reflection My mother sister cousin auntie
and home girl Let's unite in this fight Stand strong
It's Your Turn to make right what's wrong in your
life by God's anointing light It's alright Queens

It's Your Turn

Chorus: It's Your Turn to be who He called you See
from where he brought you He'll never leave you
It's Your Turn to rise above the pain Never loose
again It's Your Turn It's Your Turn It's Your Turn

Prayer
For the Afflicted

"I'm weak, Lord my soul yearns for your strength. I'm hurting and only your love can heal me and make me who you called me to be. My ways have led me astray and I'm lost now. On the outside I'm smiling but no one sees that I'm bleeding. Lord, Help me. Today I surrender all I thought I knew for a glimpse of your wisdom. You are all knowing, Lord, I'm unsure if I left today where my soul would rest. Save me. I believe your Son died for my sins and rose on the third day. I may not be ready to live for you as you wish. I admit that. I'm bound and my flesh has a life of its own. I want my body back. I'm tired of them feasting on my flesh as if I were meat in a lion's den. They devour me, Lord and I'm tired. I feel so out of touch with you that I'm not even sure if you hear me. Though my faith is not strong I can only hope that you hear this prayer. This prayer of an afflicted soul. This prayer of a child who love's you but afraid to come closer due to what it'll cost me. The friends. The fun. The reputation. Open my eyes and increase my understanding to realize its not about what I'll loose but all that you have for me to gain. Peace. Love. Faith. Confidence and Courage. Help me to seek the fruits of the Spirit as opposed to those of the flesh. Your word says it leads to death. Don't let me die like this, Lord. So in my secret cries I cry out to you. Please give me the courage to stand strong for your Word. Make me an example of what your Word can do. Yes, Lord, you sent Jesus but I need an example in My life. We need an example we can feel. An example in My family. In My house. At My job, school, in My circle. I need to feel your

presence, Lord. I need you to make yourself real to ME!
Clean me up and purge me. Lord, there are things that
I'm not ready to give up. Forgive me. Have mercy on
me, Lord. I thank you for keeping me above ground.
I've been to a few funerals and cried in my soul I wept,
but Lord, I'm grateful you kept me here. It could have
been me, Lord. With HIV. It could have been me, Lord
in an accident after driving drunk, Lord God you kept
me for a reason and I thank you. Now deliver me. Peal
off the layers of sin. Peal of the bitterness and regret. The
brokenness and the low-self esteem. Peal off all things
unlike you and reveal the person I used to be. But better
than ever before. Make yourself real to my heart, Lord.
Help me to forgive. Help me to love. Help me to give to
your Kingdom. Help me to love as you love us. I need
you, Lord. I don't want to wait for an emergency to look
for you. I'm crying out now because my spirit has starved
as my flesh has over indulged in the whims of this life. I
go as I wish and do as I please. Thinking that I'm doing
what I want, but how is that when I find myself doing
things I really don't want to do. But my flesh is taking
over. Lord, deliver me from the ways of wickedness.
I love you, Lord. Thank you for loving me. Keep me,
Lord. Keep my family, Lord. I'll be the example of what
your Word can do. Purge and purify me. I surrender...
Amen"

Love for my Birthday
*7

I met you when I was too young to know what to
do with you. And you were too wild and crazy to
care. I thought the city divided us but you proved,
in your heart, I was always there. I held you and
didn't know where to place you so time let you go. I
left and wandered the world as you built yours. And
the pain we'd find, only God will ever know.
Years passed. Families built and then somewhere broken.
The gifts of life our truest treasures, God's given tokens!
I thought I was alone here. Though in a crowded room.
On the brink of a new beginning, appeared
my love, not a moment too soon!
And its crazy how you found me. How every hurt,
heartbreak and wrenching loss prepared and presented me
to you. Wounds respectfully healed by love, how beautiful!
Words can't express what your message
spoke to my heart. But if I had to guess, it
read, 'I'm back and we'll never part'…
Somewhere in the clouds lives a promise to heal. An
oath to love. Somewhere in my prayers cries for the
family I always dreamed of. And here, somewhere in
our now, is the beginning of our destiny. No matter
what was broken, I promise you the best of me.
They say when you're not looking for love, that's when
you fall. Well I was away on trip having a slap happy
ball. When I realized the party wasn't a party at all.

I was missing love…

I was sitting there thinking about who wouldn't
make it into this new era of my life. The promises
broken. Being a mother before a wife. Living
in darkness at times, feeding off strife…
I cried that night.
Yearning for a chance to try again. Learning lessons on life
through the eyes of my friends, through trials to no end,
seeking refuge in God for wounds He promised to mend.
And then,
There was you!
As casual as a 'Bless you' to a strangers Ha Chew!
"What's up" was your title. I swear that's just like you.
So cool and smooth until I read your message, then
my phone start doing the fool! I was hours and states
away. Our distance lost its power. I was back in your
moms Tracker, bumping 'All About the Benjamin's'
for hours! I was in the 'burbs waiting for you to come.
I was back where I used to be. Back when you were
used to me, before I knew myself. Before I knew
you loved me, in the midst of everything else.
That night, I held on to your words like Braille to the
blind. You, in that moment came at the perfect time.
They ask me if I partied, painted the town
red. If life granted everything my wish list
said. If it was all that I thought it'd be. I blush
to myself, thanking God, Yes indeed.
It wasn't any of that, that made this
birthday overly complete.
It's the fact I got love, your Love all over me…
For my birthday, for life, my best friend you are.
I love you, bey. Thank you for granting
me Love for my Birthday.

Broke Up But Not Broken

You left where you used to be Maybe
you got too used to me
Lovin' You
A departure with no good bye Just
makes it harder so why try
Hatin' You
The way I felt is so strong Knew deep down
it couldn't be wrong cause I was right for you
But You left
And I ask yet you still deny you're leaving
So old songs and archive text is all I have
and I'm cleaving...To my bey's remains
My pride won't let me cry
Won't let me keep asking 30 different ways
Why?
But does it matter like What would that do?
If it all adds up to me minus you
I cringe when they ask about you
but the answers on my face
When I constantly show up without you and
Love no longer lingers in this space
I blush no longer No twinkle in my eye
No excitement when my phone goes off
No need to rush a reply
You know that tingle in your nose
right before the first tear?
Well, I have that hours on end 'cause
your heart is no longer here.
With me.

No longer on us. My focus is on me. No longer hopin.'
With every promise you ever made me And on our plans
I'm now chokin.'
They're caught.
In my throat like everything I ever wanted to say.
But it's not my fault. I won't take the blame for this
downfall that's spinning my love in dismay.

It's the mystery of how and why When did
things change? What happened to you Where
was I? And no they'll never be the same...
Way they were.
Like when you touch me
I could feel your love grow
When you looked into my eyes
Your soul told me everything my love needed to know.
You loved me. I felt it. I could touch it if I tried.
Then your tone changed. Your voice distant.
You couldn't feel me 'cause you lied.

2000+ text messages and sweet voicemails I saved.
The God in me keeps me from being bitter but I
can't help but feel I was a sport you played.
But we were on the same team.
You were the muse behind my glow now
my cheeks no longer gleam...
With questions pain can't tell and only time will heal
This has a tragic undertone with a melancholy feel
A notion of disbelief after I bought into your spiel.
I believed you. You deceived me.
Now the sweet thrill of our re-union is
killed by the slow death of your loss.
You lost me.
And I knew not what this escapade would cost me

Lesson Learned. You taught me.

With secrets I vowed to keep Never let them out
Won't utter a peep.
My first…
This burns inside. Like that drop in your belly on
a frightening roller coaster ride. I'm scared of what
this will turn to. I pray to not despise you.
You could've told me Instead you showed me
and filled my ears with more lies too!
Why keep a heart If loving is not your intention?
For this reason This very reason is the cause of
Wounded heart's apprehension.
Twice. To be hurt twice.
They say love is for fools.
Silly me. No silly you for this foolish thing you'd do…
The trials The errors of love. The
things they'd have me do…
They said you looked good with me Mama said you're no
good for me. You tapped into the good, bad, business,
spiritual, comedic and even the hood in me…
And you won't even admit it Wont
admit what's so evident.
A part of me regrets I ever did it Even though the other
twin deems this Heaven sent and our fate is still golden
Do you realize the gift you're holding?
So I guess we broke up
But my heart's not broken~

Kay Mel
For God-send

This world would be less colorful eventful and frankly
boring without your smile Your energy is reflective
of a wired sugar-high child A mile you'd walk for me
to have whatever I need And being your only child it
wasn't easy to see the sacrifices it took to keep up a life
that changed in an hour But with that unspoken power,
Mama worked it out! It's no doubt we spat and have our
ways on off days but its US! You and me baby! You are
the picture of grace sophistication and a true Lady They
call you crazy and my favorite; Kay-os (chaos) or what
about Meaux Mella, where'd they get these names?
You're a bag full of life and a
treasure full of games! I know I give you grief about your
hair, your weight, the way you ask a million questions
and talk to my friends more than me But its funny how I
have big natural hair, wish I was thicker, am intelligently
inquisitive and call all your friends when I land in the
city! You are the reason for everything good that I am I
am in awe over you Your strength is admirable indeed
but mama, its ok to cry It's not bad if you grieve or even
show that you need...Somebody. Sometimes. But I guess
You know you! No one can measure their life's downfalls
next to what you've been through I couldn't begin to
imagine life without a mother The slow painful loss of
a father My God My God-send how beautiful you are,
by far the picture of what I can only hope to grow into
How one can come out victoriously after all your hearts
been through. And you teach me well and I listen.
Though I'm grown and have made my own

way I still look to you for guidance acceptance
and hope you think I'm doing OK.
It's so much to tell you I mean we basically grew up
together There are times when I look back and say 'we
been through hell together!' But you tried to shield me
from it Thought you could buy me the world Thought
is was easy to feed clothe and bathe a cute lil girl But it
got ruff A bit complicated and even worse when our lines
got crossed I didn't know you did it all for me To have
a good life at any cost But I really just wanted you there
I always wanted my daddy I couldn't understand how
a bond could be broken so badly by those who had me
Had me thinking it was your fault Pity wouldn't let me
blame him Never could blame him So bitterness eroded
and combined with misplaced aggravation its no surprise
I conveniently exploded And you watched me Helplessly
watched me and only knew to pray When I veered off so
far off You were lost when I went astray But you never
let me go Proclaimed the devil cant have your only child
Mama you never let me go And your love is what kept me
The power of God within You say you lack 'mothers wit'
Ma how do you think you gave me wisdom Taught
me things about love sex men money life cars clothes
school work living well and making Jesus my friend?
This is why, Ma, I sincerely call you my God-send

Holding God's Hand...

I'm. REACHING!...
Searching for the comfort I yearn for.
With the mistakes I make, its a wonder I don't learn more.
So I'm asking when and why? I try to do right
wishing evil leave me. Loosing a winning
fight, living a truth that deceives me.
I'm. REACHING!...
But my past won't let me go. I left them, how'd they
find me? How did they know... I'm still weak there.
I'm still broken, bruised battered and conflicted. These
wounds? Don't feel bad. Mostly self-inflicted. And they
love it when I fall. Its more down there than above.
More giving me numbing agents than simply offering
a hug. More wishing I fail when they root me to win.
More associates for life than life's true friends.
I'm. REACHING!...
Because I know what God said. About me, who I'm to
be. With my arms above my head, the enemy under
my feet. No matter what I did, my sin is not me. I
am not who I once was. He's already delivered me!
I'm. REACHING!...
Knowing they don't want to let me go. The depths
of my turmoil is a place I dare not go. They want
me for the promise He gave to my life. I'm reaching
for God's hand because what I left wasn't right.
I'm. REACHING!...

Her Atonement
For Kayann

In secrets never revealed and a pain I never
imagined I'd feel a void all too real and the
opportunity to present my spiel...
She told me her faults about the drugs the
girl the hotel the things she'll never say
She expressed how she was told of the right
path but somehow was lead astray

How can she make amends with sins that wont bend
They broke her
Clipped her wings and those 'rings' virtually choked her
But she's better now she's okay
She can breathe and release
All things that took hold of her

It's time to let go of all things you've come to know
About me It's really not who I am I'm not that callous
I'm not that cold
I'm hurting indeed I have a smile but all the while I bleed
I'm acting out my pain and rehearsing what I saw on TV
It's not me
But sin that dwells inside 'It's ok, I'm alright'
was what I repeated in my guise
"Not you"
I can't even look into my own eyes
"Don't call me by that name its Kayn Got it Then good."
She told me she wanted out but
couldn't see her life without...

But its over and she's healed she's delivered
and inspired to live and forgive

I asked her what now? Where to and How shall this flow?
She told me the whereabouts of her
destiny is a place she longed to go
That her giving up her ways to take a route she didn't
know was the only place her smile could return
with the re-appearance of her glow
She said,
"I gave Him my life because I didn't know
what to do with it without Him
I prayed and cried out for mercy and when He delivered
me I vowed that with my life I'd pay His Kingdom.
I lost a life and now vow to live my best one yet. The
secrets I've never told are the memories my heart will
never forget and regret is not an action I take part in.
There are things in my soul that only the Lord can pardon.
So in my atonement I give up me for
the things I've committed
And never a liar or false witness if it's true that
I did it then so be it and let that be that.
I've made amends with myself and can
now decipher crap from facts..."
So before I let her leave I was curious if she'll
ever return. I mean, was it really all that bad? I
asked if she ever misses the fun she once had.
"A sacrifice is giving up what you want
to keep for yourself. I no longer have to
numb myself, dumb down myself...
I'm ok with self today." I smiled and let her
go as she lay down and faded away.

In my atonement I realize who I am and this knowledge

forces me to act on who God made me. I know why
my wrongs never really felt right. Why the numbing
agents never lifted me to new heights. I remained low
in spirit and heavy in heart. How'd I cling to so many
of the wrong things and dreaded when we'd part.
Light in love and incomplete in my efforts.
But I'm finished.
I'm complete. I'm, today, in this moment, loving Kayann.
Yes, we all remember Kayn and wished we could've
loved her and embraced her and given her the love
she so desperately sought; places where love would
never call home. How we wished we could've gave
her stability and preventing her urge to roam. How
she remained the center of attention but continuously
felt alone. It's ok. I promise. I've given her a proper
departure and together we've made a reciprocal peace.

She is who I used to be and I'm today who she longs to be.
Atoned. Forgiven. The biggest sacrifice was me...

Lost, Home

'Growing up I came to my own conclusions.' Mother
worked too much Father addiction to illusions. At
this tender young age caught in life's confusions,
couldn't help thinking there simply was no solution.
Then things got worse! Home burned down, the explosion
of hurt. I felt a burst of my heart break as a kid, and
that drove me berserk. At that time in that day in that
fire alone. I lost my attachment to life when I lost my
home. They bought me new clothes and donated toys.
New shoes to match jackets to mask the decoy. Father
about to leave. Mother too proud to grieve. Daughter
lost in the cross-fire while she silently bleeds…
So I grew up and then stronger. Never uttering my pain.
Found a home with my pen, my pad the umbrella for
rain. Rain hard sometimes other times a sweet shower.
It was here I found my strength to go on another hour.
It's really not a cliché when I say I write for life. I live
breathe and love here, call me the penman's wife! I later
found God though He never left me alone. He gave
me refuge in my talent after loosing my home. Queen
roaming with no throne, sad sight to see. Stabilized in
my words when my bags were all they'd see. Me leaving
here from there headed anywhere but here. I cried the
last time I left, thought it was where I'm supposed to be.
With my Sun by my side and a fresh journey on hand.
Guess I'm good no matter where, in life I may land…
So long as I keep writing, know I'm never alone.
For here, I'm never lost. Here, I'm home.

His View

He watched her as she fell He's known her for years
Knows her all too well But as he watched her This fall
this time He himself was too weak and couldn't help
So he stood there in sorrow He watched her from afar
though he's loved only her since God placed her in his
heart But she Oh She's a roamer flowing however she may
She wants so much more than he can do and ever say So
she passed him Year after another one She picked him up
when they dropped her off until she got her flight back
after he nurtured her back to health So he watched her
And she knew this would have to stop some day She felt
if he really loved her then he'd somehow make a way But
she blocked him She stopped him when he was ready to
bare his all And this time this last time it was him who
took the fall She's tired of coming for temporary trips His
heart can't take it He can't have her They both needed to
realize this This thing was beautiful and could have been
great but she wants more So much more More than his
life could make And her path in life a bit different indeed
She just couldn't see how the two could be and He well he
believed that love is all it takes But she on the other hand
knows it's not her fate To settle to simply give in It's risky
surely risky and apparently she's lost a friend He can't see
her She's out of sight It may burn but as bee's love honey
This sting is only right

A Page from the Journal I Swear By

There are secrets Real secrets that my lips may never tell
But these pages Journal pages know them all too well
And if you read this and then ask me
Well
I could never lie
But I'll never repeat them
No never repeat them
Read on and you'll never ask Why.

A baby girl broken
A woman's heart shattered by pain
A man who lost his way
A family in a storm of thunder's rain...
Where do we go now?
If love is no longer at home
She found work
He found drugs
Baby left lost to aimlessly roam
Woman never really recovered No never tried love
again She lost the love of her life Not just her husband
but also her best friend And him Oh the troubles The
troubles his life would see He later found his way In
a far away place away from his family The baby? No
longer a girl grew to have major issues of her own
Like how her vision of a family love and marriage
could be destroyed ruined done away with so badly
She never wanted one of her own...
But secrets are secrets to be kept only in remembrance
But it's real like I feel it like its closer to hearts distance
These are pages My journals pages

I'm willing to share a few
Share with you these secrets

That I will never ever share with you...

She was touched as a child
Vulnerable and trusting
Till she was touched as a child
Now callous and untrusting
Many men around but none came to her rescue
Keep quite She never kept quiet
She's bold and will fail you if you ever let her test you
She's in control now
No man will ever hurt her
Ok with being a mistress now so a husband can't desert
Her...

Secrets
Me and these secrets
Secrets my lips will never tell
But these secrets are secrets indeed that my life knows
All too well
So read on it gets better, that's what you like to hear, Like
carnivores on meat, we'll feed on the weakness of a peer...

I wrote about who I write for
But it was all about Me
I know
I know you'll go back and check facts and wonder
How can that really be
I put it in these pages that many may never see
Even I didn't think I'd write it
So if I become a Real Estate mogul/Writer/Business
woman There'll be some who said 'I knew it'

But most doubtful used to be me
She told me I was afraid of success
Another said my wings were clipped
One vowed I do not know the power I hold
Until now Yes until now
I've WOWed myself with this!
I believe them all though insightfully bold
But it was in these pages that I sought my soul
Pages of my secrets no ear can ever hold
And I've learned enough to know
Which things are better left unsaid Like sleeping with
two men in one night in the same bed but different hours
When you're subject to an adverse spirit You yield
to that power That flesh That busy deceitful flesh
seeks to destroy abolish and devour The very good
in you All the love that you can be But these things
These reckless things will harden your heart and
stealthily steal your sanity But those are secrets
Hurtful secrets that only these pages have read
I'll never tell No never tell But these things were
too much Much to much for my head...
He was rich married and bleeding
Had this that and more of them too
But when he met her will never forget her
For the things they'd soon go through
She was young and had spunk
A certain style that pleased his eyes
He told her things
Aching things that hid behind his guise
Fast-forward a few seasons add on a few grand
A secret
She's pregnant
Oh my! Now what's a girl to do?

Grow up Be grown 'it never happened' tell none
but she wondered what would mama do...

Oh the damage of a secret and the wicked places
they roam How they're so juicy Oh so guilty
They make your mouth their home
Cause like 'the one that got away'
In your heart they just couldn't stay
You had to tell it Let it go
For the best secrets in life surely eat you alive
Beat around the truth as you strive to say it without telling
To release this filth
This hurtful filth is at times so compelling
But these are secrets my little secrets that will never
Cross my lips If you think you've found yourself here or
think they're mine it's fine They will never cross my lips...
Here's a page from a journal that you will never read
Many actors One life and the author's always Me

Milk-Man
For D-J

"Say I I I I I I the Milk-Man, the Milk-Man!"

They say breast milk is the best milk and I thought, 'only
the best for my baby' So here's to you Milk-Man, who's
thicker than molasses and home-made country gravy!

When you were born you just stared at me You
just focused into my eyes When you came out
I said He's beautiful with tear-filled eyes...I was
in love at first sight I mean How could I not be.
A L.O.M.O and there was none to stop me!

I nursed you for the first time at 8am and you literally
slept the entire day! I can't believe it still can't believe it
that God shined brightly on me in such an awesome way!

So I went through the shaky chills and cold
sweats and figured you'd had enough to last, but
when I realized you cared not of my ills, I mean,
you didn't let an hour without nursing pass!

So for 13 months I was your source, Your Mima! A
language only we understand. Your Mima indeed I'll
always be and you'll forever be my Milk-Man ;)

Naked But Not Nude

I'm naked with you I'm exposed yet clothed
I'm Naked but not Nude
I've disclosed my inner most abode to you
I'm supposed to be cold I'm Naked
You found who I am because you showed me You
I am by far smitten
I'm Naked but you won't touch me
Just verbally
I'm Naked in words
You hold the wardrobe of my Life in your ears
Your mind pins the threads of my pain
The patches of my passions The pattern
to my everlasting desire
I'm Naked but not Nude
If this were a show of fashions in memories
you'd be the longest interlude
I'm Naked but not Nude All because of you
Who closed one eye to my flaws
Widened your horizons to listen to my
down falls and still look up to me
It's because of this that I'm Naked
Here I stand but not Nude
It's the way I'm armed w/protection but vulnerable to You
Exclusive & Selective
Yet allowed your smile to get through
The inner core of me because you
expect so much more of me
I can get dressed for hours and yet I'm Naked to You
You see the same beauty in me as God does
Dare I go there? But it's true

by A Comeaux

I'm Naked but not Nude and only to You
It's as if my love was adorned with chiffon
and my thoughts wrapped in Saran
Only to you who can see my future
with a transparent gland
You understand where I've been and
today can see where I'm going
I'm Naked but Not nude
Today it's my Spirit that keeps me glowing
Not Nude but clothed in You
Yes I'm covered and hidden in fact
I'm Naked True Bare
I'm here Yes and My Love is still
there Where it needs to be
When life doubted my success you
someway not only believed in me
But virtually perceived that We could be won
W-O-N and
O-N-E
One
I'm Naked
Two
But not Nude
And only your heart can see my life through You

All Dressed Up w/Nowhere to Go

For Kayn

"An hour, hour and a half. Yeah that should be enough time. Enough? Plenty! See all I have to do is get up. But. I'm still highdrunk from last night. Yeah but an hour is enough. To wash last night off. My face. Last night's mascara. Contacts dipped in solution only for a minute to let my eyes breathe only for a minute. Ok. Forty five minutes. Cool. Yeah I can't go without the contacts most people believe are real. Mostly me. Face? Check. My body? Um, ok, take a shower get their spit off my neck, ears, their seed out of my womb. Douche. Yeah that'll get it. Ok. Half an hour. I can make it to...To...? To...? Class, right! School, ok, I'm good. Wet and Go hair. Bet. Top? Last weeks perfume but not smokey. Jeans? Worn but not dirty, dirty. Cool. Girl, those are some bad boots! I know one thing, I be clean when I step on the scene, I mean, for school, right, class. Ok. 10 min. 10 min? How will I get there and be there in 10 minutes? Cab? 30 minute wait. My homegirl already there. Train? Yeah right. Not with this outfit. How do I go from VIP less than 4 hours ago and then get on a train? Not me! Um. Um... Buddy already left. Gladly! How will I get there? Why'd I even wake up if I didn't know how I would get there. How'd I think I was gonna get there. What was I thinking? Oh, I meant to call the cab. I was distracted by a phone call from some lost soul thinking I had the answer to their desires hunger. Though I try, I regretfully admit I can't please'em all. Man, I meant to call it before I took that shower. That's what happened. Ok. So. Now what? Go late? I can't. Won't let me in.

Then if I still go, I'll have missed the most important class and that's all I have. The other one doesn't really count. I mean, it counts, but I pretty much know the end result of that one. Try again next year. Where's my phone. Call the queens and tell them to scoop me. Let's do lunch and blow some money....Voicemail. Well, I'm dressed. Eyes in. Lashes long. I'm dressed up with nowhere to go...."

"We're finally going out. Like in public where there will be people in the room besides me and him. Maybe a movie would be nice. Grab a bite. I gotta make sure my lipglass is beamin! I mean, it's been almost two months since we've been, um, how do you say bedroom buddies in a nice way? But it's cool. Tonight we're going out. He said it. He told me we're going out tonight. I will certainly be the best dressed to impress in the spot. He'll see why we should go out All the time! I might even pay. I haven't been outside all day. I slept with my good cream on my face and I haven't let my pedicured feet touch the floor. I'm in my 4 ½ inch stilettos tonight and I don't want anything disturbing my strut. Ringer on Loud. Jams playing to get me ampd' for the night. It's 7:30 and he'll be here by 9. I literally waited to get ready. I laid here and thought, daydreamed, and fantasized just to pass time. I want to be ready just in time. Not early and never late. But when he turns on my block I'll be just spritzing the 5th squirt of perfume. The one he likes. My clothes have been laid out for 5 hours. Shoes standing at attention under my jeans. I'll put those on last. I've been waiting to wear this top. Classy yet sexy. Not a club shirt. It's a 'look at my woman, but don't look too hard' shirt. And these are the jeans that fit me in all the right places. Hair freshly tracked up. Now the lips. Eyes. Matching VS undies and bra. Top. Jeans. Fresh piece of gum. Now

a video... Call. No answer. 3rd video. Ok. Wait... 9:30!
Where did time go? No missed calls. No new text. Get
the house phone to make sure nothings wrong with
my cell. Nope. Call. No answer. Call. Call. Call. Call.
Voicemail. Not a nasty one. I don't want him to get
mad at me. What if something happened. I mean why
else would I be...Dressed up with Nowhere to go?"

Ever took so long to dress that you missed the party?
Ever spent all you had to impress when the notice was
hardly? Why is it that we value the name on our jeans
more than our own? Like renting everything from bags,
boots, men and even our home? Just so we can dress fresh
for the moment. Is it really our time or does low self-
esteem own it? What we pay to 'feel' good is a fleeting
desire, when our souls are malnourished and our highs
get us no higher. It just doesn't have the same thrill!
Dressed up depression, stressed out selection, leads to a
path of messed up direction. Who are you? And what are
you saying? By the actions of your inner ills, what's your
soul displaying? I can ask this because I can answer it.
With my head clear, mind clean. NOW, I can dress to
then nines, on time when I step on the scene. And it didn't
cost my soul a dime because I'm ok, today, with me...
Dress your heart with love, your mind with
confidence and your body with class.

I Now Know...

No matter where I go, I'll always take Me, along.
I am the best example of anything
I wish someone else was.
I cannot change the past, people, or my body-type.
A man will be a dog to a queen or a king to a tramp.
Love isn't fair. It's a poison we cannot live w/or w/o.
The more money I have. The more money I want.
God really really really really really loves me despite...
Time will surely reveal all, no need to watch it pass.
Children do what they see, not what they're told.
I can never measure another's pain to mine.
I can never predict how one will handle their heartbreak.
Yes, I now know pain pills don't heal heartache!
And no, there's nothing louder than
the shatter of a heartbreak!
I now know that a mother's love is the cure for all ills.
That a father's absence is the greatest void
next to the one only God can fill.
I now know my worth is determined by Me,
by the God that resides in and loves Me.
I now know that life will go on with
or without my permission.
Death is a part of life, it Never gets easier.
I now know what out of sight out of mind feels like.
I now know why Single Mothers are the strongest
creatures on this planet. Thanx dead beats!
My strength comes from another's weakness;
I'm grateful I rose to the occasion.
I now know endurance means to keep
going when you can't go any longer.

That when you're called to love, you'll see just
how ready or wounded you really are.
I now know God really is the only way;
Even though we constantly try to find our own route...
I now know it may seem easier to leave than to
stay and work it out, but sticking things through
builds better character than leaving ever will!
I now know the traits of a real man.
The power of love.
The weight of a woman's shoulders.
The confusion of a child in the middle of a war.
I now know the burden to succeed
is simply the fuel of success.
I now know things ignored seldom go
away without leaving a trace.
People will treat you how You treat you.
I now know, "I'm sorry" does wonders for an offense.
"I love you" saves bleeding hearts.
"I need you" shows both humility
and strength simultaneously.
"Ok" can end an argument instantly!
I now know that Prayer really really really works!
I now know the value of my name.
The importance of my word.
The weight of my influence.
The gift of my mind.
I now know that in a world of excessive poverty
and unimaginable wealth-Anything is possible!

Man

Stand up Man why watch life go pass by Why you settle
for the untruth and rather believe a lie Why you act as if
this life you were given was a curse instead of the Blessing
you need to be a Man Stand tall and stop stressing over
what you don't have and what you just can't grab Hold
your head instead and relish on those things that you
in fact have To be grateful for I'm sure there's a kid
somewhere Waiting for You to be a Man for you to Stand
and be who God made you a Leader Teacher Example
Father Brother it was no mistake when He made you
Strong and Determined Powerful and Secure He gave
you all the tools you need to succeed with an intent so
Pure to grow and to build and to create and to live The
life He promised you Man please stand Please stand Man
please be a Man But you'd rather chase paper Rather call
those a hater who try to tell you about your duties and
you act like they hate ya but Man you're a Man Why
leave women to be a daddy Maybe you didn't have one so
you know not how to be a daddy? No excuse, Man be all
things you never had All it takes is one to show up Give
love to be a dad Man sometimes I can't stand you Man
I get so frustrated for real Man you built this land with
your bare hands Think how good building a home can
feel You're a Man and God deals directly with you No
matter what we do God called Adam's name Just like He's
calling out to you You're the head of these households that
perpetuate the no-daddy syndrome Girls with no daddy
have babies with no daddy Son's with no father father
children and don't even bother To be a Man and take
that stand and yes there's exceptions to every rule There's

exceptions true enough I'm one I pray my son is But this all is too much Man aren't you a Man why let your name go in vain Why let society write you off like running ink in the rain Why let the children suffer your pain cause you wouldn't allow God to heal you Man please stand Man take your stand Please stop running from your pain and face it head on Man you're built of warriors with mighty hearts and heads strong Man you are envied and you know not your power You hold power you hold war you hold peace you hold love you hold life Man please stand and grab a woman by the hand Lead Man Please Man be a mentor to a child Man be a brother Be a son and make your mother proud Read a book Write your story Tell your truth no matter how gory You're a man it's ok to be weak Just don't turn it into pity Man Seek God find your purpose Open your ears and go with me Man let's leave here This place of complacency and lack Man get up dust yourself off Get your name back Man Strong Man Leader of the home Man get your directions and no longer aimlessly roam Man Please man Stand man Please stand There are children who will mimic you What will you teach them man Man You're a man Stand please Stand tall Man you are everything even when you feel you're nothing at all The world may be on your shoulders but God has your back Find your home Man stand please and when your lost He'll lead you back Man please stand There are too few fulfilling the duty Stop looking for a woman's worth in the size of her booty Man grow up Seek knowledge Learn to be true to self Man Please stand for there really is no one else That can do what you do Been through what you have Man Please stand Use this moment and let it not pass...Stand Man

In These Days
For Kayn

In these days I shed tears wondering why am I still here
I still fear myself due to the destruction that I've caused
To my heart mind and body tatted telling stories of my
falls And I pray at night and I know my mama praying too
But I go against her will doing what she raised
me not to and It's not who but what
and I wonder how But when
Will my heart be peaceful and I see my inner love again
I can't win this battle I fight internally
With my left brain vs. my right and at times
my flesh be burning me
It wouldn't surprise me if my hope ended up
in an infirmary But that's all I have left
Hope
For a better day find a better way
where my tears haven't wept When I've
slept and nightmares have never crept
In these days I look forward to brighter ones and I've felt
hard love now I yearn for a lighter one I'm a fighter and a
lot of things and my neck is still bound by a lot of rings
But I'm still here
To keep going To keep growing In these days
I seek a knowledge of free knowing
To finally learn a lesson that won't cost me
Thought you had me locked down, not now, you lost me...

For Him to Leave

I get it now I just got it now I know what the issue is
It all started when he told me she nag too much Talk
down to him too much That she too strong Too mean
too controlling and through his eyes she'll never see
That the two were too opposite to ever be...

And this was reason enough for him to leave

I changed for him I'd change for them So long as they
stayed and didn't leave I'd never say 'No' in the blind
hope for them to cleave To me And never leave

Never cause drama and never cause pain Be nothing
like my mama and from leaving they'll refrain Go
along with the program even if I don't agree At
least you'll be able to say, 'He's still with me!'

I let them touch me and change my life
I gave up on tradition and chose an alternate wife
Because
I didn't want them to leave
Me alone
I didn't answer to my own name and wore colors and
stripes for a team that wasn't intended to be my game

To play

But I wanted so badly for 'them' to stay
'They' 'her' 'him'

by A Comeaux

I vowed to be the most loyal friend
The low-downest chic
I promised myself to forget myself
Until I no longer knew myself and mastered their ways-
The length I'd go to for them to stay
All to say
'Don't leave like he did
I won't be like she is'
I'll quiet my voice and give up my choice
Until I could go on no longer
Until the push and pull of depression grew stronger
My spirit yearned and I answered the hunger
To live a better life than I was living
To understand real love is reciprocal
And doesn't only require me giving-
My all
Them giving me hell
Me taking what could I get
Chilling secrets I'll never tell
So I Wrote Prayed Cried Moved
Back and left again
Still broken Still wounded knowing this had to
Somehow has to come to an end

and the conclusion I came to was this...

If it hurts me to please you
If me loving me grieves you
If I can love me better than and prove that
my self-esteem doesn't need you...

Then do what they did and by all means
Leave too!!

I now know I'm the best example of how to love me
Watch me
How I'm honest with myself
How I'm loyal to my God
How I walk in integrity and live by a moral code
Watch me
Be content with me while I'm alone but never lonely
Love myself better than...
Watch me love Me and be ok if

You leave

I can say 'No' now and not care who'll tell you 'Yes'
I live a life now that's not fueled by pleasing 'who'
No drama and no stress
It's ok if you leave
Really I'm ok with that
Of all those who left

I'm far beyond pleased that I now have my daddy back

To Outlive

Pardon this sidebar off the topic and on record I guess.
My Pastor gave me some swell advice A few lessons in life
on the abundance of wisdom and the lack of stress...

He told me to watch a person if like them, Don't
touch but watch with my spiritual eye. Believe
them when they show me who they are and don't
allow my emotions to support their lie.

He told me to serve God long enough for my life to be
established on His word and from here He will bless
me. But I must be stable. Get stable and stay stable.
Due to my past lack of endurance this is a
feat I've yet to be able to overcome...

The idea to outrun go beyond outlast and see past
Today
Temptation
This moment
This trial
This hour of weakness knowing Joy comes in the....
The hurdle between hurt and recovery
To not live on a splurge of a moment
But to outlive
Outlive temporary satisfactions to avoid long term pain

His Love's Like

His love's like getting paid with no taxes
or bills to pay, yeah like that.
Like, when you're weak and can't go on
His love's like a ride with no fare.
It's something like a free pass when you flat
broke and no one to call, like that.
His love's like a gift that you didn't know you
wanted, got it and no name attached.
Like that. His love's like that. You can't see touch or
smell it but it's the best feeling in the world. It's the
kind of love that you look for in others but He's the
only one with it. He'll give it to you if you exchange
your ways for His. It's a sweet deal if you think about
it. Really, no comparison. His love's like the best thing
my life has ever had. And when I grow weary and give
my hope love and attention to another, He's forgiving
and more nurturing than a newborn's mother.
Like that. His love is like that. Like that void that only
He can fill. That space in your life that money can't
spend, clothes can't fit and sex won't fulfill. Like that.
His love is like that. He placed it there; a space where,
when you're ready, He'll put a smile in your heart when
nothings funny. Like that. He made that hole, that
empty place we go through life trying to fill in His place.
Nothing works. I'm talking to those battling their souls
in church and still feel 'something' just don't work...
Like that. That thing you won't surrender. You want
Him to heal the sick, forgive the sins, but you're not
ready to give up the lust that lives within. I know.
That's how I know His love's like that. He has the

answers our mouths don't have the courage to ask. His
love's like surreal but better than that. It keeps you. It
heals. And guides those led astray back. His love's like
home. Not the broken one. Or the shattered one. But
the home of your heart. Yes, like that. His love's like
the only thing good in us after a life of hard times. His
love's like that far off ray of light that radiantly shines
and leads us...Back home. It's by His love that defeated
Queens retrieve their throne. Like that. Its like that. It's
how slaves remain undaunted and become Kings of great
lands. His love's like incredible. Its incredible how we
lie cheat steal kill backslide come back backslide leave
backstab backbite and He love us back. Home. Love Us.
His love is like the mother that some never had. The father
others never knew. Its the family a few went without.
Its like an assuring comfort when we all go through!
His love's like nothing. Not a thing to compare. It's a
love that surpasses all love. Surpassed by all love, too.
His love's like the way we should love each other.
His love's like the way you should love You. It's like
never ending time. It's like a love that's all mine. But
He has enough to share with the whole world.
His loves like the way out of hell that saved this little girl.

An Ode to the Lost

They watch us as we wander.
Wander through life wondering, "Why am
I Here and if I'll ever get There?"
Where they say I'm supposed to be.
I'm opposed to being 'normal' and do things as 'they'.
I move to my own waves flowing however I may.
I'm lost to them.
But to me, in my eyes, I'm smart
enough to know-'this' aint it.
There's more to life. Than a cubicle, a
dog and being 'anymans' wife.
If it takes me 5 more cities and 10 more
years, to find myself and true happiness I
will have surpassed that of my peers.
See they think we're lost.
Those silly fools.
They have no idea, a free spirit RULES!!
God hears me and he draws near to my call.
Yes, I fail and though undaunted,
even wandering souls fall.
But I rise in the wake of depression
and on weak knees I crawl.
I'm a survivor.
A mother with a precious seed who looks to me
to give him all and everything he needs.
How must I wander when stable he needs to be? I know.
I know.
More than anything he needs ME!!
So I sit. And be still.
Wondering if again I'll wander.

I seek to find my purpose; a thing
or two I constantly ponder.
But to those so free, I say, "Roam on my friend." For the
journey to find Self shall never in this lifetime, end.
We're ever changing beings.
With love coming and watching it go.
Learning lessons daily, especially
those we think we know....
Life is a trip!
Renew your passport, please. Never hinder the
spirit. For this will cause the heart to grieve.
For this is my Ode. To the beautiful wandering souls.
You know there's something missing, opportunity
presents itself, then there you go!! Take pictures.
Phone home.
And remember those left behind.
Please know, fellow wanderers, you
can never leave You, behind.
The world will only Show you things, Its
up to you to find what's inside.
I'll watch you from my window.
For my Sun needs me now.
I've found what I've been searching for;
at least of course, for now....

R.I.P.
Robert "Big Bob" Eugene
1935-2005

My Soldier...

As read at his funeral 12/31/2005 by Kayann

Dear Grandaddy,

I been struggling with this since I got the news and though I told you the last time I saw you You were the Best Grandaddy I ever could've had. I have 25 years of fond memories, lessons learned and a whole lot of, "Hello!" when you made your point. I remember my first fishing trip, my daddy brought me along as a 'surprise buddy' and I had the time of my life! From then on I appreciated the serenity of the water and how you found peace. Fishin'. Each time I think of each school you drove me to from Louisiana to Michigan to Atlanta, I think to myself, You a Soldier!. You were a father to those who didn't have one and a mother to the motherless. You were a friend to the friendless. And I'm grateful to God that I had the chance to even KNOW you! Let alone be loved by and nurtured by you. They just don't make men like you anymore Grandaddy. I pray my son has a touch of your spirit and a heart half your size. If so, he'll be phenomenal. And though he'll never comb your hair or sit on your lap and play with your bushy eyebrows, You'll live in my heart with each beat and each breath I'll remind him how great a man you were. Too bad I didn't learn how to cook like you. But we'll talk. I trust, as always, you'll be there when I need you. You always asked me, "Are you listening?" Yes, Grandaddy, I'll be listening for you for the rest of my life. You were a Soldier, Grandaddy. But these bodies get sick and grow weary and pass away but everyone here today knows an angel lies before them. We each have our own testimony of what your legacy means and it's a beautiful, beautiful thing. I'm sorry to see you go the way you did but honestly you're doing a lot better than all of us down here. You were a Soldier but God said struggle no more. Fight no more. Cry and yearn for love no more. Suffer no more. Relax and fish all day. As a Guardian Angel guide me, touch me to let me know it's 'ok'. Fear no more. Worry or be weary no more. Stand Strong Soldier. These bodies return to dirt. You loved hard until it hurt but it's ok now Soldier, nothing can harm you any longer. I love you from the depths of my soul Gdaddy. You loving me made me stronger...

Intro to
A Paradox: Prose of Love and Lack thereof
…a collection of stories w/complimenting poetry

"…Pastor told me, 'You can fall in love with a dog'… That's heavy. Think about when you loved someone and never knew them. How you never got head but religiously blew them and caught more than your share of hell when you were faithful keep your mouth closed for no defense and legs open to ease any suspense and even when granted a night wish as he lay there you feel the distance. It makes me wonder who you love more. If you screwing another woman's man for money you're still a glorified whore and if you're screwing a man who broke too then you aught aim for more…

Love will lead your life if your heart has peace or make you the queen of deceit and run you up and down like city streets. Careful where your heart leads you, you'll take your soul body and spirit and all those who need you. Your body will buy a life your spirit can't afford and your flesh is never full and will always yearn for more… Careful…"

As you prepare yourself for the paradox, walk softly for my journey is a bit unorthodox. Learned more from mistakes in the course of hard knocks than was ever taught in school! Raised smarter than my ways blinded by another mother's fool, I can only say this now that I'm through! So read. Grow. Close your eyes and admit you were there and no one will ever know. Still writing for you and these characters are a peace of mine two…

by A Comeaux

Falon's Story
From Bliss to Betrayal
-The Man He Loves
-One Word

Jessop and Jessona's Story
Touched by man, Touched by God
        -Filling Potholes
        -Mourning Cry's

The Waters All I Know
'Where is Your Love?' Ciara speaks
        -I Vow
        -Here, Say

When Every Shoe Fits
But Nothing Feels Right-My Story
        -Mama's Baby
        -Letter to Sun
        -His Roll Dawg

Falon's Story

"Good morning!" She beamed as she kissed Riley on his forehead. He's not a morning person but this is was a special sleepover. Dating for over a year, she's certainly beyond in love! He's wounded. Emotionally scarred from a marriage gone wrong. But right now he's sleeping. Hungover from 'partying like rock stars' the night before. He's sweet, charismatic, funny and has indelible sex appeal. The public confirms they look good together. Yet he has a secret that will break her. But for now he'll let her love him. Like crazy! He feels its about time someone proved themselves worthy of his attention and affection. A woman who'd lick his wounds and asked nothing in return was ideal. Just be happy to be with him. That'll have to be enough for her. All he needs is a band-aid, a crutch, really. He's a firm believer that by this time in life, you love who you love. And anyone new is a waste of time or a time waster. But Falon? She's a good girl with doting parents who celebrated their 35th Anniversary the weekend she graduated with her Masters. The only daughter, youngest of 3 and a text-book Daddy's girl. Any man's prize. Women are all the same in different ways. She wants what most women want, except she by far is worth her weight and she knows it. No baggage, intelligent, beautiful, understanding and independent, with just enough vulnerability to allow the man of her heart to lead. Falon has had her share of hot dates and seasonal loves. But at this point, in this season, she's spent enough time alone to know herself, heal wounds and accomplish things love would've distracted her from. She always wanted to add more to a relationship than her body! For a man to see her as a nurturer for their kids, a vixen for his passion and a partner in life.

She wanted to be 'The Package'. Not perfect, but acquire the needed attributes for a successful union with the man deserving of all that she is and looks to be. And when she met Riley, her heart literally skipped a beat. He was almost shy and stalled at her initial 'hello'. He was taken aback. Their attractions chemistry was palpable with stares that spoke louder than his honey-kissed baritone once he mustered the needed air to reply. She cracked a mega-watt smile to break the ice as he looked away blushing at himself for being so boyish. But he liked it. He hadn't had butterflies in what seemed to be a lifetime. He was granted another chance by love's hand. And she was more than ready, more than willing to give love her best shot yet... Riley thought Falon was cool. Easy going and funny. Lovable and accommodating. Cute enough to make others jealous, even without make up which he found a rarity these days. His ex-wife would be envious. If she cared. The two will never cross paths. Falon will never know of his unspoken life. She'll never know where he was really from and he'll never take her to meet his *real* mother, not even the one who raised him after the incident... Yes, he has secrets. But today, 5 seasons into the relationship she's dubbed 'the one', the man in her heart, body and mind is the man she loves. Completely. Even if she doesn't know who he is. So as he snores, she realizes she's bored. So she'll cook! She's got a mean breakfast game and he'll surely wake up for that! Subtle buzz. "Where's that coming from?" She goes about her ambition to knock his socks off with her omelet and waffle combo. *Buzz.* "How do you turn on this radio? Where does he keep his pans, griddle, condiments, I need some direction around here! He sure has plenty of utensils and gadgets to be a bachelor!" She spoke out loud. But only the designer cookware heard her. She worked her way around that kitchen like Rachelle Raye. *Buzz.* "What is that damn buzzing!?" As the warm aroma of Columbian coffee filled the air, she sizzled an omelet worthy of a photo complimented by homemade cinnamon induced waffles and turkey sausage her mother would be proud of. This plate was beautiful. Just like the smile he'd put on her heart. Who wouldn't want a smart beautiful woman making breakfast in bed? 'He'll love this', she thought as she blushed to herself. He's snoring still when she returns to his room. Breakfast tray in hand. *Buzz*. Its his cell phone. She places the tray down to add the cell phone to the smorgasbord of goodies she'd created for him. *Buzz*. She stands frozen. Waiting to hear exactly where its coming from. Nothing. "Damnit!" She picks the tray back up and continues over to her new love. Sleeping so tenderly, loudly, but sweetly indeed. "Babylove! Oh Babylove!" She croons with sunshine in her tone. No one or any silly buzzing was to keep her from her King! She paused. Took a moment to soak up this monument. As she looked around the room, for the first time. She noticed she'd never seen it in daylight. How the sheets complimented the shams and curtains. How each tone took a note from the other. The night light next to the headstand for evening reading. The flat screen on the wall she'd never watched a movie on but was sure that was next. The desk over on the east wall where she assumed he'd paid bills on his expensive laptop and maybe read the paper. The throw rug and matching pillows now on the floor, but still looked exquisite. He had taste. Expensive, chic and she'd wondered if a woman had a hand in the birth of this ensemble. She watched him sleep. And time stood still. Bare, caramel kissed skin. Forearms strong, gripping the extra pillow he can't sleep without and that she couldn't replace with her body. She wished she was that pillow. She will be. She'll be his comfort that his life can't live without. One day. He's come so far. It took her a while to get him to see that its ok to give her his heart. She wasn't sure what the last woman did but she was certain it was bad. Maybe even unbearable. He'd been through a lot. She could tell by the look in his eyes. A look of fear and hurt and a yearning she couldn't put her finger on. 'What do you need?' She wanted to ask, but didn't want to pry. 'He'll come around', she thought. He'll see I'm not like 'them'. He can trust me. And he sees that now. Hopefully. But she's vowed to be there for him in any and every way a good woman is supposed to. *Buzz.* "That's it!! I'm finding that annoying phone!!" She'll regret this later. In life, like in years to come. She'll wish she didn't hear it. The buzz. That voice. That call, that text, that woman doctor talking about that man. As he lay there. Sleeping so beautifully while she discovered his coveted nightmare. His past has yet again risen. And while he sleeps, his nightmare speaks. Riley was molested. As a boy through his teen years. And somehow the disgusting secret of his youth became the fetish he couldn't explain. Or live without. When his birth mother could no longer deny his being violated, he was placed with a distant Aunt who he dubbed his mother to his new friends. His new life. And he never looked back. Not even to Fran, his own mother. She sent him to college and out into the real world never speaking of 'the incident'. He went through life never addressing his hurt, his confusion, his secret desires. Yet, he took a lover once in a while. He called them "episodes". Times when he yearned nothing more than the strong forbidden grasp of a man's love. The very thing he hated, the one thing his soul loathed was the one thing his fleshed burned for. With a beautiful wife and two sons the spitting image of his handsome features and his wife's warm smile. He had it all. On the surface, but there was an itch he had to, didn't want to, but needed to scratch. His wife discovered this secret the hard way. She was the only woman he'd ever loved outside of his mother and her outrage surprised him. One fateful night, he'd confessed to her the ills of his childhood. She held him as she shed tears for him. A good man, the love of her life, father of her children, cried for the childhood he never had. Sure she would love him more. For the mother he hadn't seen in too many years. For the family he's detached from. She held him and together they wailed. Cried out their pain. He never admitted the episodes. She found that out on her own. He understood her hurt but for her to leave like that, after all, she knew about his childhood. She was his best friend and he only told this story, in its entirety, once. They shed tears of pain and confusion and hope and bonded in ways intimacy for either of them had never known. 'How the hell could she leave him after a night like that?' He retorted. He hadn't had an 'episode' in years. And when she found out he'd willingly violated their vows, no explanation would do. She and their two boys flew across country and he only gets to see them when she seldom visits, though he pays both spousal and child support, this is the extent of the life he longed for for so many years. He thought she was beautiful. Smart and classy. Nurturing and witty. Independent and accommodating. He married Taylor without ever thinking twice. Pure, honest love that he hadn't felt since, well, never! He felt safer with her than he did with his own mother. And she was gone now. His life was gone. Children gone. His heart was gone. *Buzz*. What Falon read and what Falon heard broke Falon down. 'Auto Accident. Emergency contact. No other known relatives'. But her man. Her King. The man she'd been having incredibly passionate unprotected sex with. Lay there so peacefully not knowing that yet another wonderful woman was on her way out of his life for good due to a secret that haunts him. That he hunts for. And he's the prey. Or the prowler, depending on the day. The doctor said his lover may not make it. That he'd been asking for Riley since he was in the ambulance. That he needed to tell him something. Riley lied telling him he'd be out of town for the weekend but Mr. Gresham begged the doctors to please locate him. 'Yes, this was a matter of life and death,' he'd implored. The doctor asked Falon if she was his sister, aunt or relative. Exactly who was Falon, she asked, before disclosing confidential information. "I'm his sister and he's sleeping." She mustered the air to talk. Her heart caught between her lungs and the rage that was maturing in her mind. "I'm about to kill this bastard!" 'Excuse me?' the doctor inquired. In her theatre trained tone of cordiality, she shook off her intentions saying, "No, nothing, doctor, Um, I, uh, will wake Riley and get him to call you back immediately. Thank you for calling and let Mr. Gresham know Riley will be there soon." She's not sure if it was the phone crashing into the door or which plate shattering the window above his head that finally woke him. Maybe it was her heart breaking that broke the silence. Every plate, cup, each dish made from love now attributed to the rooms décor. But broken glass seemed like shredded paper next to the vengeance he saw in her eyes. He didn't have to ask. Her discovery was apparent and he never got upset by the storm he'd awoke to. Something in him knew. Though they had never met, that was the same look in Taylor's eyes. His head dropped. He didn't know how and frankly it wasn't important. He knew she knew. "Mr. Gresham is in the hospital. You're the emergency contact on his insurance. He's not doing well and has unyieldingly requested your presence." All this said with the same tone they taught her to use when she wanted to scream but words would be more efficient. This tone said, 'As soon as I get these words out something bad will happen because with each syllable the fury is growing and I can feel a fire pit in my gut!' Hence, the grittiness of each word provided just enough gravel to make this thee most uncomfortable scene in life. Her discovery now turned to concern and even though he tried to mask his initial reaction, it was at this moment Falon knew Riley loved this hospitalized demon. Not because he's her man's lover, but because in this one morning, one act, this one phone call, this text that read, "Please answer, its an emergency!" This one breakfast that now only a good mopping will feast on. The meal now being adorned by the walls and windows, all destroyed her desires of ever cooking, or proverbially love again, it was over. For good. For her. For real. How deceptive? How wrong? What did she miss? What signs didn't she heed? "Damn you!" Her eyes warned she was homicidal. Riley, head down, wanting to get up and rush out of the room. To the shower to think. To the hospital to support. And ask why the hell did he do something like this! To get in his car to just ride with no destination. But he couldn't move. Tired of running to and away from this. From himself. So he sat there. And cried. For Falon. The sweetest woman he'd ran across and who he'd given a fair share of hell to just to make sure she was worthy. Of what? To end up betrayed. He's been nursing a broken heart for longer than he's been loved. And for the 2nd time, he's seeing the toxin of his past ruin his future. His family. His life as a whole. So he cried. He called Taylor's name though she was nowhere in sight. He screamed his apologies to his sons but only the walls received them. And Fran, he only screamed 'why'!! Why mom, why?' Its the saddest groan from the soul of a grown man grieving. Loss. Of direction and love and peace all due to these things being robbed of him when he was too young to understand and now too accustomed to change. Riley sat in his shattered breakfast, in his shattered life, in his shattered heart, for what seemed like hours. He never heard her heels screech, never heard her 'goodbye', never heard the door slam, or the car's engine. He never heard anything as loud as his life

shattering. Again. But this time he knew the under currents of his life were making waves that were drowning him......
Buzzzzz...

In her car. She sped from the driveway as if someone, some evil flesh eating thing was chasing her and the only super power she had was her acceleration pedal. So she sped. Only her eyes filled with too many tears to see. Each wipe caused her to swerve. Each sob made her illegally cross a lane. "HONK"!! Fear and nervousness and the sheer will to want to die in this very moment took over her. 'The baby' she remembered. "NOOO"!! So she pulled over, if you consider running up the side walk after disregarding a curb, as pulling over. And she cried. Punched her stomach and pulled her hair. Anything to make the outside hurt as bad as the inside. Inside she felt her heart dissolving as if it were doused with acid. Her heart was gone. Leaving at least. Falon was 3 months pregnant. Completely elated and hadn't told anyone yet. This was the cause of her secret celebration. She took him to Ruth's Chris and told him to order away. Drink for her because she couldn't indulge. He never even questioned why. Now he'll never know. How could she bring a child into the world with a father who's not really a man? How could she love a child and hate, completely hate the seed from which it came? Unfair. To all involved. If she aborts, how will she look at herself? This is what she's always wanted. If she doesn't she'll be living the biggest lie in history. Who could she tell? Her best friends had eluded her. Her mother wouldn't support, well, either decision. Her father would be so hurt he wouldn't be able to look at her. "NOOOO" She screamed as her voice shrieked across the windshield and bounced off the windows. And Riley? He'd better not so much as dial her number. She was tempted to go to the police and cry rape. Get him locked up where he belonged. Perfectly fitting. 'KNOCK KNOCK'. There was a man in his mid-fifties staring at her as if he were witnessing an alien abduction. 'Huh? Oh, yes, sir I'm fine', she mustered. "Ma'am you're on my lawn." She looked around like she'd fell asleep and woke up in another life. But this was real. And she had some real decisions to make. First was to get off this nice mans perfectly manicured lawn. Second see a doctor. Or whatever you call those people who fixed conceptual mistakes in the privacy of a clinic affixed with protestors. Wonder if they still do that. Protest? Who could rally to keep a child from a man who's, well, another mans man. NOOO!! "Ma'am, do you need me to call someone? You don't look well." *Theatre time.* 'Yes, I'm fine, I only lost my way. My phone, my coffee spilled on my lap. Ummm sorry. Here.' She hurriedly grabbed an unaccounted for sum of hundreds from her purse and while he looked puzzled, he accepted. In the same motion, whipped her face and put the car in gear. 'Highway.' Leaving the memory, the hope and the attempt of love alone for good. Maybe she'd take that position she was offered in Japan. But love? Never again. Never the butt of life's joke. Goodbye love. It was nice. But this is the end of us. And honestly, the end of me as the world knows it...

by A Comeaux

The Man He Loves

To live and to die for. In loves truth and to lie for. Something's can no more be explained than they can be understood. Can't be right for you no more than they're good for anyone who dared you would. Love. And deceive like the song crooned. That this thing will make you do right and wrong too. That you can be fulfilled while one constantly longs for you and your desire, like the Bible promised, is never fulfilled. Like sweet tender innocence maliciously killed, the oppressor is somewhere in his dead spirit deliciously thrilled. And the man he loves will never look at him the same. His own seed never thought to bring such shame. To think this all started with a cold hearted game. If its one then it's the same. Spirit. Silent cries that they live by but only kindred spirits hear it and their inner demons fear it because they might change. They hate this. Like the sweet consumption of the forbidden fruit, they rot from the inside due to the fact they ate this. They die internally far longer before their faces sink in and eyes roll back. It's a path they took, daddy, shook and know he can't go back. Where? Home? Where the violation started? Where he and his manhood innocently parted? Never! And though his secret silently creeps in, it's a stench in his soul he quietly sleeps in and who's to say who'll claim his spirit? When the induction of this cycle was forced, the inner groaning of the man he loves is the only one who'll hear it...

One Word

I'm crawling from where I ran to. Bruised by what I cherished. Betrayed by who I believed in and I'm still asking why when its here in my face where you used to be.

Absence.

In place of you is the face of who I used to know in the place of which I used to go but I'm lost so there's no use to show. Up.

Depressed.

I heard, 'No' but your eyes muffled my ears and now they're ringing with last nights cries and vision now blurred with last years lies that today I see truth but. Damn. It's with the removal of you.

Moonshine.

If it's the only light I see like the tunnel and I'm dying here. This is dead but living without you is like my thoughts with no head no direction no one to tell them where to go no one to keep them no place for them to gather and be dispersed accordingly and allocated to the appropriate individual at an appreciated time...

Ok. So you're gone. Right side. Bed cold. Head hurts at nightfall like clockwork. Your chores left undone. Old toothbrush, almost empty deodorant, your dingy socks and a faded t-shirt. Wont throw away or discard. Maybe you'll need them one day. And if you come back and those things, those menial things are gone that would speak volumes like loudly speak. I didn't believe in you. In us. This. So I keep them as if this will jinx you to come back. Or maybe just remind me that you were here and this isn't the sweetest dream I ever lived that turned into a nightmare that I can't awake from.

However did my life come to this? This cold place is like no place, and because it never happened I'm more than numb to this. No. This never happened, it's just a bad dream. Burn the pictures, block the memory. Love is never what it seems. Never what it's supposed to be. How could I be so far from the truth when you were so close to me? So here I come world. Minus the heart I was loving with. The breath that I was breathing with and eyes I was seeing with. It died inside as the seed I once carried. It died with my dream book and fantasy ever to be married. Its dead like you are and no I don't remember your name. I only recall the season that it poured after it rained. One word. Lie. One word. Kill. One word to soothe this. One word. Pill. One life. Gone. 3 lives affected. 5th life absent. Last one infected. One word. Gone.

Jessop and Jessona's Story

Mother

"Dear Lord, I ask you forgive my sins, both knowingly and those subconscious. Those old and new so that I may get closer to you. Dear Lord, please bless my mind with peace, my body with health and my life with joy. Please dear Lord, never let your hand leave my life, for I need you each day in all ways. In my speech, in my thoughts, in my actions and deeds alike. I need you, dear Lord. I thank you for the love you have bestowed upon my life, through a mother and father richly loving and nurturing me. A protecting brother and best friend, Jessop. A home safe and all our own. I thank you dear Lord. I love you more than I could ever prove but I'm dedicated to show you. In your precious son's name I pray, Amen..." She prayed these words, these very words each night. Aloud. As if she were praying to these walls, these thin walls than couldn't keep a secret to save a life. Jessona has always been favorable to things unknown, unseen and beyond her unversed understanding. A dear neighbor asked if she may accompany their daughter for a play at our local prayer house, and I found no harm in it, and ever since that day you'd think the girl was a minister-child since birth. Harold and I were never big on the whole 'holy' thing. We worked, did right, raised our children to be kind and respectful and figured if there was a God he'd be happy with just that. I mean sure there's a thing bigger than man alone, but we never paid much mind in figuring it out. Being right by our twins is the most valuable notion of spiritual reciprocity we could ever offer. Now Jessop? Well he's a story. More handsome than big Harold could ever dream of but not nearly half the man in character or stature. Seems his low self-esteem makes him appear smaller. One would expect so much more from the first male child of his generation, at least on Harold's side. We Brewshard's are plenty in men! That Jessop is simply a looker. He's good to look at as he looks by as life passes him. Simply wants nothing much, and won't work for it if so. I'm too old to badger him and too tired to notice most days. Except nights I hear him weeping. A weak, subtle but sincere groaning I hear from his quarters. Room not far from mine, to keep eye on the boy. But a few hours before dawns bright eyes, I hear his tickle of a cry so muffled seem like its unjustified. What's the point in crying if you can't get a good moaning out? By breakfast hour he's back to normal, back to mum. We don't ask. Guess we both know. Since Harold left, whole house been a bit more quiet than I can say I ever remember. That Jessona carries on like she works for the Lord himself. Gone most of the week and all day. Dinner as a family and I don't care who praises what. We eat as one and will do so til there aint but one of us left. And when that happens, well lucky one, do as you wish. Like an East sunset, there are some things that aren't to change. Harold was our glue. Our anchor and protector. And that hour is what we called ours for as long as we've been a family. Sudden change, sudden death, sudden things happen that leave indelible marks on life that time, well hours, can't claim and won't ever fix this heartbreak of mine. Least not healed completely, maybe numbed the ache. Or stagnated the burn. But still broken. Harold was my life's only love. My only friend. He taught me to drive, cook and sew. His mother a seamstress. He was the reason I became a mother, in soul I wanted as many replicas of him nature would allow. After the twins my woman parts gave out. He was pleased to have a son. I cursed the heavens. Since they say that's where babies come from anyhow. No mind. We made a beautiful life for the twins. And until Harold's health showed wavering strength, we were the strongest unit known to our bloodline. He was a great father. A real stand up guy. Died in his sleep. The morning he and Jessop were to fish. Jessop found him. He lay there with his father until the doctor came. Until the morgue took ole Harry's body from us and we never seen it again. I don't bother with all that. They delivered his remains. I keep him in a respectful space, but nowhere that'll haunt me. Except nights. I love my boy, just don't know how to help him. Help him be strong, be a man and fearless out in the world. Old Harold was doing a grand job with him before he was snatched from my grasp. From my life. From my hearts only soul. That Jessop seems lost without his dad as if he never had one. Boy knows he's supposed to be out there making a living for himself, starting a family of his own. Stead he sits here mourning the one he lost. Me? Well I'm already old and done what I was put to. Guess I wait my turn to hear my name. Hope its peaceful. Old Harold left in not so much as a whimper. I kissed him when I was off to make a lunch for their fishing trip, he felt part cool, such a fool I am. Kissing a dead man I didn't know wasn't alive anymore. Maybe could've helped. Brought him back. Told him living aint living without him and love aint home no more. Maybe asked him to hold on. Wait. Take me too. Just wished I could've said something other than try to bring some salmon instead of walleye the night before. Poor man died with only a fish request from his wife. Silly woman I am. No one here to send our Jessona off in the wild event she's asked in marriage. Girl thinks everyman is a product of satans seed. Said they're 'flesh eaters' and I at first thought she'd caught something. Something eating her alive. Until I realized the poor girl has sworn off men, love, anything outside of worship. It's a lonely life without love, lonely to the heart and starving to the soul. Having no one to love. No one to share this cruel and unpredictable life with. And my Jessop wont touch a girl either. Wont court that sweet girl from high school who's had eyes for him since 3rd grade. Precious thing she is. He treats her as if she's carrying the plague. No opportunity for new life. No grandchildren to sit and watch giggle. No new life in this place. And the old one is gone far from here. Old Harold took our lives with him when we lost him to time. Time took him. That Jessop worries me. Jessona ignores me. And Harold left me. What exactly do I have to wake for? We eat dinner and they scatter like roaches with the lights on right after. I usually don't mind much, actually. We only stare at each other the whole time as if we all just met. Making small talk and asking asinine questions we've all memorized answers to. *Get through the moment. Get through dinner. Get through with life. One hour at a time.* I, most nights glance at his rocker that has a thickening layer of dust accumulating. The television set mostly off. Usually just watched what he watched. And that couch offered down from his parents when we were first starting out still standing. Still covered in worn fabric. Still smells like my Harold. Jessona say she prays for me. Jessop tells me he'll never leave. That's by default I'm sure. Where else will he go and to whom will he allow to watch him sulk through life. I hear him near the whispers of my window chime. I weeps with Jessop. An immature grieve with an over-grown hurt. I hold my breath, my tears in my finger tips so no one knows. And once in a while, I let one slip. On bad days, on days I missed him so much I can taste his scent in my mouth. And then I hear an echo. He mirrors my moan as if that's how he knows its ok. Its to cry, to loath life in the midst of living it. As if its unfair for us to be here without him. What air did Harold breathe that choked him? And why didn't we gag until now? I think. Maybe its him listening to my cries…

Jessona

I think they burned clocks like all sense of time when they burned daddy. That's what they did. Mama just let him get burned all the way up and now he sits in a jar far up top of her closet. That woman. She stopped living when he did. And time hasn't passed in her eyes since. Jessop either. They both wake up and wait for night to sleep. Or weep really. As if in darkness is the only place grieving is allowed. I cry everyday. To my Lord God. Yes I do. And it feels like He gives me a power and a strength I never had. Never had here, in this old house and older memories. I remember when he first touched me. In the stealth of the midnight hours with his strong ruff hands, sour spit and forceful grip. Since a tender girl. He's the same size as daddy. Smells the same. I always wanted to touch his face, that's a sure difference. A sure way to know for sure. But my hands always busy. Plugging my ears. Covering my eyes though my lids sealed shut. My mouth. I cover my groans and cries with the salty grip of my palm. But I wish, always wish I would scratch his face. Memorize the sharp features with my fingertips. A part never wanted to know. Never knew to hate for sure. So I despise them both in the privacy of my thoughts. Two polar opposites otherwise. Loving, and accommodating generally. But dark and devouring after sun set. But I never knew the difference. Still can't tell. Jessop is weak. Afraid of the outside worlds rejection. So he rejects himself and feeds off his own self misery. He feels if he loathes himself, us hating him would be less hurtful. I perfectly hate him. For taking my innocence or never protecting it. Either way, he's guilty and my only prayer is for him to choke on his tears and die quietly.

I want to leave, live up top of the church. Maintain the grounds for Pastor and never have to ride that hot sticky bus 6 days a week and twice 3 days. Regardless of his filth, I miss my daddy. He made me laugh and taught me about men, more so than that Jessop. We're twins but its like I don't know the boy. But only I understand him. He's afraid of his own power. He's always been taller, more handsome and smarter than most kids in his class. Just to fit in he stopped doing his lessons. Made himself just about dumb just to fit in. Except, well, he never did. Guessing he never will. At least when daddy was here he's try to perk up some. Help fix something. Get dirty. Lie about a girl he met on the way home from a place he didn't even visit. Just to make conversation with daddy. And ma? She just walks around, nibbles and asks me why I'm always at the church house so much. Where else should I be? Here watching folks alive act as if they dead. We are all dead without love. My love was taken from me long before I ever left my front yard, so the world automatically looks better than home. I know they love me. But now that he's gone, daddy I mean, its like everyone misses him so much they cant enjoy a good nights sleep. It's the first time I've slept in years. And now they cry all night like Santa himself died. These folks! I wonder if I'm a virgin. Church folks take great concern with if you've ever been touched or not. Never told them. I'm not sure if that counts. No one ever asked me you know, to touch me. I never looked in his eyes and consented. It was a perfunctory agreement that I suffered through until I found solace in his humiliation. Assuming he was as humiliated as me, and the misery continued. Each morning I'd search their eyes, looking for guilt, pleasure fulfilled, something!

Blank. Both of them. Like they witnessed a hanging and simply turned the other cheek. 'Never mind another mans business.' And mothers been clueless since I met her. So that's why I've committed my body to God, since violating me wasn't enough, now they have to live with trespassing on the Holy ones territory. How's that! Let me see you explain that on Judgments Day!

by A Comeaux

Filling Potholes

"Father, forgive me for I doubt. Heal my misunderstanding over things I can't comprehend. There's sex. Drugs. Lust. And Love, which you are. These things can occupy and medicate wounds. But it's you, Lord, I choose. My father is gone but I feel him here and those left behind exists as if they no longer appear. See through. So I close my eyes to the depression in hopes to somewhere see you and, Lord, I know you care not of what rhymes but this is my heart speaking in this cold lonely time. There's no love here. Just memories and old clothes. The stale smell of yesterday and anticipated destinations with nowhere to go. But you, Lord, are the filler of potholes to make this journey a bit easier to travel. You are the glue to my sanity before my logic seeks to unravel and a path maker against distracting gravel. Fill me, Lord. For this time, this blow seems to be the hardest. This one is the coldest of all time and I can feel my home becoming heartless. And regardless 'whodunit' and the offender you'll vex. I fear I may never trust a man because of the presence of incest. Spoiled on the inside, for the pain I had to ingest. And now I seek you, Lord. Period. I'm out of things to say. I feel dirty because he touched me. MAKE IT GO AWAY. Take the resentment, brewing in my womb. Take the heartache. Take the pain from her eyes, for the truth I bet she knows. Take this life you gave and give me another one. With you. In your Kingdom, where there aren't any potholes…

Mourning Cry's

How do silent tears rumble in the night, like thunder in a storm but this seems unlike… That. She cries and then I weep. She wakes up and lies there as if she's waiting for death to seep in the room and steal her last breath she's so willingly ready to relinquish. A solemn and noble mourning versus deaths invitation grows harder and harder to distinguish. How do her tears end up on my face? How can I be the man by default when I never trained for that space? Its crowded and lonely and there's no one to lean on. Makes me sound weak when I'm the one they look to be strong. I am. I only cry when she does. One night I will go hold her and we will cry that one night as one. But when I think about doing it I'm beat by the sun. Until the next pre-dawn and its as if it's the first one. The first tear on the first night. No, these silent tears that rumble like thunder will never no Not ever feel right. Be it guilt or my own pain. Sunny shower or hailed rain, its cold here now. Under my pillow I weep but she can hear me anyhow. And my twin looks at me funny. But my height affords me to see past it. But her gaze is piercing to my soul like hells fire promises never to be outlasted. I'm not sure if I'm more afraid to live, like this or die. She never had a shot here, and me? I never tried. With examples to learn from, no protection to save from harm. She's cold and detached because even her home wasn't safe from harm. Not sure if I hate him more, or mother or my own reflection. I hope she leaves and never returns and takes her life in the right direction. My mourning cry is for her…

The Waters All I Know...
'Where is Your Love?' Ciara speaks

The water, the calm serenity of its stillness moves me. I'm amazed at how something so beautiful, so fun and exciting, so important, mystifies and soothes me. So refreshing to the soul yet so devastating and powerful. With the ability to destroy anything in its path, it's an intriguing paradox, Love. Water, seemingly so simple, yet vital to our very existence...

'So there's this guy! Yeah, I know, there's always a guy, but this one, I really like. This one is not like the others, this one stirs me up all while calming me down. He can cut me with truth and bandage it with understanding all in one sentence. This one walks it, the parting of his lips unnecessary. He is genuine, yet confused, eons removed from being malicious, yet still manages to make it hurt. Shows affection, yet the bricks come down slower than I would like, wise in his decisions with still so much to experience and learn. He gives me what he thinks I can handle. Yet I'm a full-time worker, and temporary gratification is insufficient.
And knowing all of this has my heart in a state of confusion. Treading in uncommon territory, mind wondering:
Do I ride the wave or get out of the water?...'

It's dark and its cold here. Once you delve in the tide. It was warm and inviting, enticed to come inside. They were laughing and playing and frolicking about. Leisurely tossing love hereto, inside and out. I guess I wanted to play there. Found a soft spot in his sun and decided to stay there. Oh, the view from where I sit! With just enough shade yet perfectly lit. Yep, folks, I think this is it! So I began to come closer. No fear here, you see. They coaxed me, befriended me, as innocent as can be. I'm coming, I see you. But see I've drowned once before. Life jackets on board, yet the deep end I seldom explore. Its safe here, right? Close to the shore. But it truly, feels like I'm missing something when I want so much more. Is that the sun setting? Already? Seems like I just arrived! Now its getting dark and young loves must return inside. But me? I'm no novice. I can handle my own weight. It's the unknown that entraps me, for I know not loves fate. Toes first, here I come! I can see your hands in the dark. I can feel your fear for me falling somewhere deep in my heart. But its ok, somehow. I think its safe even in storm. This being completely new to me, yet feels like my norm. Feels crisp and warm. Cold and hot at the same time. Tapped into the inner core of me and revived my main line at the same time leaving idle. To wonder why the waters so still. Only to be awakened by wave flustered with emotion. To remind this is real. This is now. This is the wave of loves water right now. Still. Yet always in motion, its alive! Its living breathing positioning itself somewhere deep inside. And I ran, but the water, like love, is everywhere. In every language and every color it's the only place where, well, we all can relate. Can't live without either of the two. Be it a walk on the beach, or storms come and blew. So long as I ride this wave of love with you...

'But honestly, I love the water. Even though many around me abstain from entering and decide to watch from a distance, it's not enough to keep me away. Even though it's tricky; sun shining bright so your mind says it's perfect on sight alone, but the initial contact forces you to prove your allegiance.

It's not as inviting as you assume, therefore you must emerge yourself completely, in order to get used to the temperature. Cold or not, that doesn't change my feelings. I still love the water. Even when I swallow it, eyes bloodshot red, throat sore from choking, unable to catch my breath...I love it... Even though I know that there is a good possibility that the very spot I'm standing in, someone has decided to use in place of a bathroom. I'm loving it. Even when a piece of marsh brushes against my foot and my mind reacts as if it's Jaws himself. I'm still loving the water. Even though I know that I'll be itchy, sand stuck to me, toes and fingers will be all wrinkly. There's no better place I'd rather be...

I remember my first dive. In love, in the ocean. The same one that said, 'its ok, I got you'. Was same voice I heard underwater screaming, 'Its not you'. I think I lost my breath when I first lost my love. But how can you avoid the very things you dream of. It took a minute, maybe a year, to get my courage back to swim. To try to float or even enter into the water again. Flashbacks! It can happen, again if you're not careful. But I learned inner love on the way to the Lake and God said this is what its there for. To love me when someone else may have lost my heart at sea. To pull my belongings in my beach bag and leave that boat to be. Yes its cold and even lonely when there's no arms to hold my heart. But its here that I continue to heal until I'm shot with cupid's dart...

How ironic that I'm comfortable here, despite the fear, the tribulations, the uncertainties.....It just feels right. In my heart, my spirit, my mind. It's like old friends getting together, laughing and catching up on missed events. It's like riding a bike. It's like coming home to the comforts of my bed after a long weekend away. Naturally beautiful like hair in a messy ponytail, jogging pants, no make-up, clean quiet house, popcorn and my favorite movie. Kinda like overhearing another person say you're beautiful, not aware that you were listening. It's like embracing that special someone, forcing time and distance to no longer exist. My body's used to the temperature now, I feel like I can do this all day. I love the water!

I embrace, you love, dear old friend. Looking back at the sweet beginnings and heart-wrenching ends. The beauty of my first dive, how the adrenaline made me feel alive and the numbness of the cold made my tender soul cry. I couldn't get around it. Grateful for the revelation but regretting that I found it. All at once. Afraid and eager. Bold and insecure. Certain and confused. All these things, love, I feel still today. Each time the season comes around that emotions seek to play. Each time the sun shines in such a dark place. I remember you, love. And learned to embrace your storms. Like when best friends fight sending off hurricanes alarm. I cry for you, love. And miss you when you're gone. In those seasons the oceans froze only the memory to keep me warm. I need you love, for the power you give me. In the laps of life I can only ask you forgive me. When I left I didn't tell you, I was too hurt to stay. When I ran from you, love, knowing you were the only way. Who can live without love? No more than one can live without water. It's the saddest thing watching a broken heart to the slaughter. You watched me bleed, and grieve from wounds inflicted upon myself. You watched me with tears in your eyes when I loved someone else. Like the calm before the storm, when it rained it poured. But it was because you loved me that those times we endured. They say we fear that which we don't understand. Well I'll spend my life trying to stay afloat with your heart in my hands...

So I will continue to be fascinated by it's beauty, the mystique of the unknown, just waiting to reveal itself. I will not be afraid...to swim, to indulge, to play! To be purposely lackadaisical in my approach, floating amiss the surface, waiting in anticipation of what's to come next. It's an intriguing paradox...Love. Water. Seemingly simple, yet vital to our very existence.

Ever seen a thunderstorm? Ever felt one rumble within your heart feeling your joy and happiness part? This is what happens when you leave. This is what happens when in my soul I grieve. I need you love, my truth, but you relentlessly deceive. Damn that drowned me! Took my heart and threw it and only darkness found me with no softer than vultures around me! Love, right? Is this you holding me or is this my sorrow fitting hug-tight? I stop breathing when I'm under your currents and I can only hold back for so long. I can't stay down for my perseverance provokes my spirit to be strong. Let go of you or die and hold on. Live in our memory or embrace the day without you and move on. Here I am, love. I'm still watching you from afar. I'm watching you though you can't see me... Look up an hour past midnight above the ocean, I'm still your star.

I Vow

You are the very heart of me and with every part of me I vow to give you the very best of me Compromise and accommodation is the biggest test of me You'll come 2nd to none next to God My love I vow you can have the rest of me. You're beautiful. And I'll stop there. Looked low and wide for that look in your eyes and no matter who stared I realized it's not there! Here, you are by far the best love of my life. It's an understatement to call me your wife, I'm your rib. The future womb of your kids. When our eyes locked My mind popped back to '95 like 'Whoomp there it is!' There goes my baby. My Sun sans daddy and we've yet to make babies But today, I'm your lady! And we'll work all that out. Exes and hopeful next Mrs., yes we'll work all that out. Because you, are the very heart of me and with every part of me I vow to stand strong by your side. Like, if you went blind I'd give you my right eye to see Us together for the rest of our lives. I more than Love you. Yes, I see you in the mirror looking in my own eyes You're so deep In my heart My spirit and it's no surprise when I yearn for you Your soul hear it! We are Success in love and only a fool would fear it. You, Love, are the very heart of me and with every part of me I vow that for better or worse, No Not just that, Whether blessing or curse, We'll reign together. Sunshine or life's rainy weather I vow here like this now we'll reign together like how Queens do. Check mate! Triple jump, bump pawns let me King you! You are so Beautiful to me Until then like this now Only in poetry Can I express my passion for your presence and in these words you know it's me in my rawest essence My heart is open. To you and all components of all you do and if you stopped, loving me, that would be the end of time. No hours. No minutes or second chances in this love. We.

Are. Evolutional and no element of life can replace love. Yes I more than love you. You are the very heart me and with every part me I vow to give you the best of me. Your future. My love's destiny. If you love me like you say you do, then do what you said you'd never do. Be the man ordained you to. Break barriers than came before you and soar. HIGH! Take me under your wing and let's watch time fly. Nothing can move this mountain we call our love. Nothing can touch this cloud our passion is made of and they thought we wouldn't last! Silly fools. This is the very essence of the best in class. My heart is bigger than it was before. I'm much stronger than last time and can effortlessly endure. The very pain of your past and the fear of what's to come. The hurt you still remember and the thoughts still undone. The questions roaming in your mind, 'Is she really the one'? 'Each pair of legs with an open invitation, Am I really done'? 'Is she the mother-figure I need to nurture my son'? 'Can I be the father needed to raise her Sun'? Daunting. I know. But I'm willing to see. I'm willing to try and give you the best of me. The best God granted my heart be. I just pray the same for you and love doesn't elude me. You. Are the very heart of me and with every part me I vow to love you with every ounce God's willing to give me. I'll share with you. It's this time this hour this strong this power to supersede any attempts to devour. This love. I can't love without my heart. Which you are. The best part of me...

Here, Say

They say some words can't be said right. How could I say goodbye when I never knew I was leaving? When all I really needed was to get my head right. But I loved you in the rain of life when it thundered and poured and lightening shattered my hopes and damaged most of yours. I'm sorry. Not to sound cliché' but what else can I do when there's nothing more to say? Waiting for the storm to pass, to hear the soothing words on the tongues of birds the morning after. 'We made it!' With glee equal to a child's laughter. Here where they said we'd never see. That place in space of love's time of an hour of yours and an eternity of mine. Shared so there's really no space that you plus me isn't there. Here, say I love you and promise to never leave. Say you'll break my heart and watch it bleed. Say something I can believe. What weight do words bare when your actions have already beat them there. Say it! Here, say it now. Say you love me but you just don't know how. Well then tell me it's over, "CURTAIN CALL" actors bow! Tell me I came too soon, right after when you were ready, but not now... Tell me. Something my heart can take home. Tell my hope it's useless and our unit is now reduced to alone. Because, well, you simply won't love back. This push and pull for your affection is more like a war and I can't tug back. And they said we looked good together. Must've missed my cries. Must've overlooked the pain tucked sweetly behind my eyes. They didn't see the demise of my dreams or brokenness of my tries... Here, say goodbye.

Homemade

I wanna make love.

No really make it like with my two hands and your arms. For me to nurture our nest and you to protect it. Like that.

I wanna make love.

Beautifully hand made and delicate but a foundation solid. Firm. Able to withstand. Time, Temptation, Trial and life's errors. Yes.

I wanna make love.

With the swiftness of my feet and the strength of your legs. To get over hurdles and long jump past opposition. For you to carry me if I'm weak and me able to quickly catch you if you should ever fall. Never. I've got you.

I wanna make love.

With my eyes and your vision. To see your hearts desires and keep you focused on the goal. Our goal. Yours in Mine. Mine in Yours. Wanting no less than the peak of OUR success.

I wanna make love.

With my head and your thoughts. To be like minded, on one accord with decent intentions and sweet desires. To meet you and take you. To understand you and never change but grow With you. Right from where you are. And I, too, will follow suit and allow you to be You as you respect my mind and what I do. Your Yin to my Yang and eloquently accommodate you

I wanna make love.

With my body. Your soul. My spirit. Your heart.

I wanna make love.

Make it. Take something one left and Make it. Yours. Mine. Make it right. With the heavy burdens of the world with a good woman and a real man we can make it light. Because you laugh with me. I want to share my smile with you. And you can share your pain. You can be an umbrella to my worries and repel discouragements rain.

Yes.

I wanna make love.

When you love me inside first. When I know your heart. But, love, You must know You first. As do, I. Need to know your hearts truth even when your fear would force you to lie. I said, I need to know your hearts truth even when your fear would force you to lie...

But you can trust this, unknown, unexpected, unplanned and undaunted heart to love. Your weariness can find refuge in a place you've never been to but will never want to leave.

I wanna make love.

And keep your heart in mine and never let you down, no never let it break. I've been there and another heartcrack I simply can't take. That means you too. Wont break yours no not ever. I'd hand it back to you if I can't keep it. Unharmed and sweetly departed. No sadder scene than a tender love brokenhearted...

So, I apprehensively ask...

Do you?

Wanna make love, too?

When Every Shoe Fits

But Nothing Feels Right-My Story

Growing up I came to my own conclusions. My mother worked too much. My father was an addict. While education was strictly enforced, there was no one home after school to check my homework. And while I was told to stay out of the city streets, this is where I spent 90% of my childhood while my primary residence was sparsely occupied in the suburbs. My life was a paradox long before I knew what one was. I knew early on that we were different. My family. Our structure and strategies may have been unorthodox, but Ours, nonetheless. This love in dysfunction was ours. I daydreamed about being normal. But how do you simplify complexity? Can you ever untangle a spider's web? How does one understand the very thing that perplexes the originator? I simply didn't get it. What made her run from home? What pushed him to Use? Go with me. I'm about to tell you what it feels like when every shoe fits, but nothing feels right.

It's 1987 and I'm in my uncle Dub's Tracker with my daddy and we're blasting Geto Boys on I94 speeding to Grandma's on 111th St. No emergency, that's just the way he drives. He looks over at me, his best friend/baby girl, to check on me and mess up my bangs with a loving ruffle and slight muff. Another unconscious ode to his desire to have a son. But I'm loving this moment. Me and my daddy. Riding. Doing our own thing on a beautiful Saturday morning and its just us. Plus, we're matching. He matched our clothes often. That was cute to me. I guess he knew that. I know we're going to grandma's because of that tall white building at the exit off the highway. I love being on the highway with my daddy. Even to this day. But before we make it to her house, we cruise through Roseland so everyone can see us. Him, really, and I guess this truck. So he makes stops that I'm sure are unnecessary, leaving the car running, music up loud and me sitting conceited. I'm fly too, playing the role and perching my glossed lips while playing in my long pressed hair that I'm sure most adults let alone little girls simply didn't have in the 'hood. To be honest, my hair is as long as the white kids at my school. In Roseland, I have these girls beat hands down. And I know it. And they know I know it because I act like it. Plus, before he laced up my new Jordan's, he gave me all his dollar bills. Both my pockets are full of cash right now and my mom just got my hair done with a fresh Press-n-Curl last night. Please tell me who's fresher than me and my daddy? They can't touch us! This is not a special occasion. This is how we do it, daily. And weekends we really get down because I don't have school and he doesn't have to worry about forgetting to pick me up, not that he ever did. I'm his heart. It just breaks up his runs when he has to come to my school, which I secretly love. I'm instantly the most popular 2nd grader when he pulls up in a clean Cadi, gators and leather pants. He never wore jeans, until prison, so even when there's nowhere special to go, he always looked like an occasion. This is what I missed most. When he left like when he had to go away. They took my friend from me. You see, in the lonely days of being an only child, he was my buddy and I loved that. My daddy is so cool, so funny cracking the craziest jokes! Damn them for taking him away. He didn't even do anything that bad. But away he went. It was a bad day from the minute I woke up. I forgot to hang my uniform the night before and it was wrinkled in the morning, so I ironed it. And the steam released the secret that this uniform was funky. Why didn't anyone make sure my uniforms were cleaned all the time or at least make sure I had a clean one on deck? So now I have a stale stench and those Catholic school brats can be brutal at times. Then I missed my afternoon bus and the trauma of that evening never let me remember why I missed it in the first place. But when I finally found my way home to grandma's in these uncomfortable yet expensive shoes my mother so affectionately placed on my feet, assuring me that the ghetto kids would never have them and I'm sure its because ghetto mothers had common sense... I got the news. The most retarded and off-day I'd had in a long time, commenced with my aunt sitting on the couch casually relaying to me these exact words before she even asked why I was home 2 hours and 45 minutes late. I'm willing to bet no one even knew what time I was supposed to be home. But she said it and this was my introduction to depression. That low feeling in your gut that you can't even reach with ration, understanding or comprehension. So it sits in the pits of your hope and in the middle of your joy and rots because you can't grab it and contain it to break it down so you can get it. Get it? So you can look at it a little closer and try to make peace with this monster. Depression it was surely depression indeed. "Your daddy went to jail today." That's some cold stones to chew. Losing everything I had, every toy, sock and memory of my life thus far wasn't enough to loose, now my best friend is gone too! Bastards! I screamed the 'F' word into a pillow in grandma's room about a million times. Maybe 2. Until I fell asleep begging the Jesus I prayed to at school to please let this, this whole screwed up day be a bad, nasty but grateful its only, a dream. But it wasn't and when I woke up. I still smelt funny. I forgot I didn't eat so I felt sick and my daddy is nowhere around to take me for a Happy Meal. I wished there was something I could take to make me sleepy again. Years later I found it but that night, I needed to get gone. No one. Not one person ever asked me how I was or tried to comfort the confused mind that would later attempt to destroy me. He'd burned down our house. It was an apartment but he burned it down. A year earlier. Had a huge fight with my mom one morning on the way to school and me with my stupid uniform on, it was all I had left. After the fire, I mean. But I'm scared. Seriously. He begged her not to take me. He jumped on the hood of her car and she almost killed the man as she pulled from the curb with him wearing his good coat. The full length leather with the fur trim. Can't remember his outfit, though. Just him begging, "Don't take my baby, leave my baby here!" She was crying. She always cried. I just looked out of the window. I always just looked out of the window. But now my daddy is crying into the windshield and I kinda want to get out to talk to him and tell him to go back to sleep and maybe try this again tomorrow. Maybe today isn't a good day to be out here like this. Out here this bad. I can't say I wanted to stay with him. He was a bit strange that day. I mean, sure we're best friends but what's the big deal today? I go to 2nd grade every day. Why is he on the hood telling her not to take me? I'm confused. Needless to say, she took me. We left him. Maybe he was confused too. But all I know is that by the time the bell rung to release my distracted mind, my life would never be the same. They told me he was sick. That he needed help. And then they drove me to my place, what used to be my home. Now burned and soaked and useless. Everything in the joint was useless. Dollhouse from granddad. Jordan's and leathers. My furs and my pictures. Anything and all things included. My life was gone. And they said he did it. Wow. Those were some cold stones to chew.

Those years, my adolescent years were crazy. Confusing. Almost a blur now. My mother did the best she could. I mean, she lost the love of her life. Her husband and the only man she ever loved. Still. But from where I sat, this was my world turned upside down and they, all of them, had the balls to tell me to keep it together. 'Act normal.' 'Do good.' 'Be happy.' You can't possibly be serious! But they were. As was I. Too serious for a child of my years. There wasn't a lot I found to be funny. I felt as if I'd lost everything that mattered and whatever was left was ruined. She was ruined. Burned she was bruised. He was gone. And from what they told me it would be years. You know, as a kid, you never look at years. As in time, you just live and look forward to the 1st day of school, your birthday and Christmas. That's about the size of that. You don't look at it as in when you'll get your daddy back. Knowing that your life will never be as it was. She's not coming back to him. So where is home when the heart is broken?

She moved me so far from the city I could go to sleep twice and we'd still be on the highway. I tell you, highway driving with mom was a bit less eventful than those excursions with my daddy. She seemed heavy. Not in weight. In life. In spirit. Always. This had to be a living nightmare for her. I mean, she's continuously in denial. Maybe she's a chronic optimist. But this fire, this jail time, his raging addiction, the official severance of her glamorous life slapped her in the face with a cold rag and I know it hurt. Deep. Embarrassing. She worked at one of the most prestigious law firms in Chicago. Probably the envy and joke of most of her family. They wanted what she had but knew she had a problem on her hands, well, he had the problem but you get it. So now she's left here with this evil, smart-mouthed and spoiled kid that wants her daddy. Period. Everyday. NOW! But we're in the boon docks now and I'm supposed to act normal and not tell anyone about all this. 'Whatever you say mom.'

Anything to save face and not look bad in the presence of others. I've never, to this day, understood what the big deal is. Be who you are and let people deal with life as such. Why cover-up and sugar coat? Never really got that. My new step-dad was certainly weird. Beautiful house. A real house with a field for a backyard, and our kitchen and bathroom were fresh from Home and Garden. No exaggeration. And he never touched me. Hit me nor violated me. For this I'm quite grateful. Who needs to be beaten or molested on top of losing your life as you know it?! That would suck! But she couldn't marry him. She could've, but wouldn't because she didn't love him. For real. Like she did my dad. I think her heart was burned in that fire.

So we moved on and now I'm approaching high school. I'm okay now. For the most part. Kinda. At least now I'm beginning to function and go about my life. Developing new memories but I'm certainly detached. From everything. You'll see this progress later. But daddy, he's better now. I guess jail doesn't have drugs at his disposal, and he's found a religion. I visit. Mom never. Just the once to sign divorce papers. WTF! We write. He's reading and writing well now. Proud of that. But he confessed there's a love-child. Damn him. She's beautiful. Looks just like him and I'm confused. Again. I agree to meet her. And on religious weekends I can get there, we meet up at grandma's and sneak off to the Garden's where she grew up. This is fun in a scary way. The men that you'd normally be afraid of are the ones you're somehow related to and they vow if 'any fool try you they're finished!' No one ever tries us. We party. Drink cheap liquor. She smokes, weed too. This is almost as fun as when my mother used to take me to the PJ's in the '80's, the white building at my aunty house on weekends. Anyway, me and my sis had some cool weekends at grandma's. I took her around my 'hood, too, not as interesting and dangerous as the Garden's but good, clean fun. Even took her to the 'burbs for my sophomore year Homecoming. My dad, our dad, is out now and he dressed us alike and drove us all the way to the 'burbs for my dance. And everyone was impressed. She was a great dancer and pretty. Plus all the teachers flirted with my dad. That was a good night. He even dropped us to the Garden's afterward and we partied all over again! Rock star in the making. But somewhere in the midst of this, his addiction re-introduced herself. Dirty bitch! I told my mother once, when I was younger, that I didn't care if he lived in a tent, that I'd live with him. At this route, he was surely headed for one! You see, I took up for him. Always defended him. Carried his burden and never gave him problems. He's an addict. That's enough to deal with. So I gave my mother hell while shielding him like he should've protected me. But I'm strong. I can love him through and out of his addiction. No one else did. They all, at some point, gave up on him. He's a chronic 'relapser'. Can't stay clean to save his own life. Poor man. So strong yet weak in his own demise. So I figured since she, my mother, was the stronger of the two, this is who would carry my burdens. My confusions, hurts, pains and struggles would be hers, I took his, she can take mine. Still to this day.

Then he moved out of state, continued to use and I just gave up on the hope of normalcy. That just wasn't my life. At this point, marriage is a joke and children are accidents realized. No thanks on the whole order. I just want to be rich. Or happy. Happy more than rich. We always had money, and the whole damn lot was miserable. So, I'll take happy for $200 please. When he left, I guess I just wanted him to get better, again. I wanted him to get happy. It took a while but one treatment, one year it finally stuck. By this time,

I'd experimented with my sexuality, let's be honest, I was stuck caught bound and wrapped up in my confusion. For years. Call it what you wish. But I'd found my own ways to medicate my pain. Remember when I was younger and wanted to find a way to get to sleep? Found it. Everything I wanted, good bad addicting and disastrous, I found it. Like help, the alternative is always available. And if you think my daddy hurt her, imagine what this mess I'd turned into was doing to her. Disrespectful, ungrateful, and rebellious. Relentlessly. She was lost all over again. If ever found. *I'm sorry. To hurt you on top of life hurting you. I'm sorry I pacified him and punished you. I simply didn't know what to do with this. I didn't understand what an addiction would destroy. It made me inconsiderate of you when I nurtured him. I babied him. Spoke softly and loving, never wanting to add to his pain, his great deep and enormous pain that neither of us ever understood the root or end of.* What would drive a person to do this? Use. With a beautiful, virgin wife, intelligent and goal-oriented with success on her heels. We were a family, he started this unit and it pains my soul that drugs ruined my childhood. Despite the efforts others bestowed upon me, I kept a hole in my heart that ached and like a bad knee, it flares up randomly. The man who gave me life deteriorated before my eyes. My late Grandfather was a Soldier. Its no wonder his daughter, my mother, is a Warrior. She gets heat for being a beast. Still to this day. But I'd be dead without her. Her strength. Her perseverance. Her fight. Even when it hurt. Even when her blows were too strong for my broken heart. All she knows is to keep going. When she bled, when she lost, when she didn't know where her life went, she kept going. And it paid off. While most of us, her onlookers, fell victim to the undercurrents of the waves we thought we could surf through, she was on her belly kicking and paddling. Coasting now. Eating good while some starving from the over consumption of life's illusion. No matter the buck I present, you tame my opposition because more so than not, You're right! Still to this day.

And him? I never wanted to hurt him. He was already so hurt his life was bleeding. A slow mysterious leak in his spirit and it was as if he knew not from whence it came. Or how to stop it. Neither did you. Neither did I. You left him alone to figure that out. I'm not sure that was best, but you obviously had your reasons. So you left me, to choose. I had to choose, mama and I'm sorry my choices were so biased but I was a child. And those ways developed, matured and still battle my heart. Still make me think you can handle my world's burdens. Still to this day. And then he finally got it. Stayed clean. Long enough to notice life. A few months in treatment and we're emailing and I'm his distant council. He confides in me. We're re-building our relationship as he's learning a new way to live. Maybe he'll come home when all this, wait, where is home? She's broken. Certainly doesn't believe in him, or love him the same for that matter. A bit bitter if you asked me. But as usual, no one does. And I guess when it comes to her pain, his pain, my pain, who's to say how we are to deal with it. Who's to say its wrong for one to act out their pain in this way or that one? How can you measure my brokenness to yours? Ok then. Life allows us all the freedom to hurt. And the choice to choose healing. The responsibility to live and the audacity to die, inside when we let our past, our failures or things that happened to us to be the result of what happens in us. So he finally chose life. And I'm grateful. He's still fragile for sure, but its ok, like I said, I've found ways to self-medicate and when all else fails, mom is the burden bearer, so I'm good. The limits and offenses of the lack of love. Come on, dad. I can handle it. He's met a woman. Good, I guess. Don't think its time. Actually, I think he should sit still a bit longer. It was just a year earlier I visited him at a woman's house for the holiday and exactly one day before I arrived, he sold everything he bought me for Christmas! Gimme a break! But I didn't utter a word. If my mother so much as didn't buy something on my request list I'd go off, big time, let alone blow an entire holiday! But with him, its almost expected. He's an addict. He's sick. He doesn't know what he's doing. Kinda like a two year old. But he's not two. And I know he loves me but this is getting old. But I go home, empty handed and give my mother hell I can't explain. She buys everything she thinks I'd like and then some. Still pissed. Bleeding even. But that was years ago. Crazy teenage years ago. And daddy, I too, have a leak in my spirit for you that I know not how to stop. But back to this woman, he says she's nice. Cooks and treats him like a king even though he lives in a shelter. I'm grown now, but... Seriously? My mother would never have that! Wouldn't look twice at him or any other man for that matter in such a condition. Still to this day. All I said was I hope he's happy, please stay clean, and if she makes him relapse, God forbid, I'd be to see her. If I'm here, muffling my life's blues in fear of him carrying the very burden he put on me, keeping quiet when all I wanted to do is tell him what this, all this, and these years have done to me inside, if I'm bridling my tongue and my pain and fear and discontent to shield him from those provoking demons that lurk within him so he doesn't use on my behalf and she comes along, brings some drama and messes with his oh so fragile mind and he Uses. Yes, I will be to see her. But he never used. 10 years and counting. Praise God. And while I cried during his entire wedding. It was too soon. She's not who I would've picked. Her family, her everything, no, why, damn! But ok. I wont say a word. So long as he's happy. Clean more than anything, I'm good. Still to this day. I'm ok with his choices. Because the most important one is for him to have never used. I know he's not happy overall. But he won't use no matter what. And low and behold, we found out he has another daughter. Honestly, I always envisioned somehow, I'd get my daddy back. To myself. On the highway, cruisin' through town. But that's selfish and even God said it's not good for man to be alone. And the baby, she'll have what me or my sister never did, a childhood filled with a father, clean and involved. Everyday. He gets to be a hero to a little girl saved from a life of abuse. He saved her. Look at God! He promised to restore that which the enemy destroyed. He has. I'm grateful. Really. His wife has helped him raise a little girl she didn't give birth to and never treated her like a step-child. While their marriage at times has caused my ulcers to flare up, he's never used. And everything else is secondary. Not ever using. These are his choices and today I'm grateful that while he's made some stupid ones, the most important one has not changed. He won't use no matter what. No matter who. That's all I ever wanted. And now, finally, he can carry me. Yes, I can call him crying, and tell him there is a major problem in my life, that I'm in trouble, today, I can tell him that I need him. Need him to show up for me, my son, my anything and you better know as sure as I carried his, my daddy will pick that problem up and annihilate it with a vengeance. He's a King finally at his throne. Sure I wish he would've spent more time with himself to learn his ways and flaws without the involvement of another. This is his choice. Be it as it may. Its his addiction that's affected me. His addiction planted a seed of void in my life that stole memories I will never recover. I never told him these things. I acted out my pain, and let them figure out why. It was a lack of love that lead me into most pits I was buried in. I didn't have his hugs, his authority, his presence as a disciplinarian. I went from being cared for and catered to, to being his support system. I knew he needed me, but I needed him. His addiction and its hurricane superseded my childhood. Consuming me. Shattering what I knew of love and my life at that point. Yet still, I had his back then and I have his back no matter what. Still to this day.

I'm living today. Yes, we all know I'm alive, thank heavens, but I'm actually living! While I hold an immeasurable amount of love for my daddy, I've released him to God. I no longer fear for his sobriety or his life and trust that by this time, he's well enough to make the best choices for his life. And when he messes up and drops the ball, he learns from his mistakes and continues to never Use. Amazing! I adore my little sister and unlike our other one, I'm involved in her life. By the time I met her, we were already teenagers and pretty much set on the conclusions we'd made about life, our daddy and how his decisions effected us. But the little one, she's precious and has the chance neither of us do. Simply beautiful to have your daddy. Clean daddy. Aware and capable daddy. And today he can be the grandfather to my son, his namesake, that my late grandfather was to me. Today, he can teach my son things only a grandpa can and be there when I'm not and his father isn't. My life was blessed by my grandfather. His wisdom and insight, his sense of humor and his understanding. His love and discipline. And when I was lost, caught in my own confusion, needing a place to run to, each time, I now have my daddy. Clean. Aware. Protecting daddy. The first time was in 2002. I gave my life to God and simply wanted to be free from the demons I'd collected in my travels. Louisiana. Michigan. Chicago. Atlanta. OMG! Atlanta polished me off! Like a kid in a candy store with a pocket full of money, eyes full of greed, and heart full of mischief. Boy did I need my daddy. And he was there. More than anything I needed salvation. Relief. Clarity and direction. From the dope dealer that consumed me. From the dyke that confused me. From the drugs that conned me. It all looked so good. Felt right and got me through seasons, moments and sometimes simply comforted me. Yes these nasty things, were my life's friend. The friend your mother tells you to stay away from but you two have so much fun together! The friend that you can't see is about to devour you. In due time. These things I would cling to would soon be what I'd get bound by. Only God. If it had not been for my father running here first, then I would have had no place of refuge. My mother loathes, somewhere in her soul, the very fact I came here instead of home. But I needed a fresh start. Yes I know you take yourself with you when you leave but when I brought all those demons to that alter, they all had to flee. I was bound in those situations because I felt I was needed. I needed to be needed. I needed to help one who was wounded and hurt and couldn't help themselves. Sound familiar? All my relationships were surrounded by me helping, aiding, giving, relieving, nourishing another in one way or another, though compensated with whatever my demands were, there was certainly a need I was eager to provide. Carrying their life's burdens on my back. To prove myself. My love. My loyalty. Proving that I can love you when the world turns their back. Wow. That's a big one. Until God opened my eyes and allowed me to love myself, first after loving Him. And He blessed me with my Sun who consumes my entire heart. I know love, real, true love, is reciprocated. Not manipulated.

This day is beautifully flawed. As you flip these pages with the emotions I've provoked, know that I'm good today. My mother, father and myself have experienced our fair share of life's transitions these past few years. And individually, with God's help we've found our way yet still searching. A Paradox. It's all I know. I cry when it hurts and I fear it when it feels too good. Seems wrong when it's too right. Call it what you want. It's my life and no one, not him or her, can take that away from me. My mother would bare my every pain if she could. And he'd erase any memory that haunts me. If they could. But that's not it. These wounds and bleeding scars are mine. The glory is God's. 'I'm a writer and a fighter and a lot of things, and my neck still bares a lot of rings… But I'm still here. To keep growing, like my mama, I keep going!!'

I love neither of them any less and wouldn't be who I am in all my imperfect complexities which make me content in my skin where I find solace knowing No One loved and taught me more than them. By life's lessons or default, hence, A Paradox…

by A Comeaux

Mama's Baby

Mama give me clothes and nice things. Mama get my ears and finger rings. Mama take me here and all the way over there too. Mama dress me up and tell me to shut up. Mama speaks for me. Loudly. And said she believe in me but somewhere doubt me and I know in my heart that her life might've been better without me. I beg too much and I'm so mean most days. Not sure who I am and imitate his bad habits in more ways than she'd like. And like Sophia all her life she had to fight and so that makes her good at it. Defense. Always me. Where is this coming from? There it is. Somehow it surfaced. It's always, 'he'… Taking blows he couldn't duck from with wounds no one healed. Mama tell this truth and to her this is all that's true. If you oppose, here she goes, Attack on You! Mama got tear stains on her heart from all that she's been through. Wanna go? Wanna see? Mama will take you too. Baby gone now. In another zone now. But she clueless. She knew this. Still mama baby and their pain keeps them crew thick! And she holds grudges tighter than she need to and she tells your truth and seldom believe you! Never uttering the words, 'I need you…' Lost her own mother as a young lad so I guess she held the attitude, 'I need who'? But like chiffon her strength is see-thru. Her cut may be from a different cloth but it's still able to bleed thru. She's all I ever had and she knows me only in prayer. Though I left home too soon, her presence was always there. Like the comfort of an angel. The comfort you get when you know it'll be ok no matter the spoil of the day. Grown on my own still mama's baby…

Letter to Sun

I hear your cries. In nights my weeps awake me. In your eyes I see your hurt and vow to never let pain take a seat. Just a moment. 'Dear God, replace the void with love. Give him the security and direction he needs and the courage true men are made of.' Okay, Sun, see you'll be fine. Yes, you're his son too but see here in this spirit of time, You Are Mine. My blood in your veins, my milk kept you alive and my prayers made your tender spirit thrive. 'Hallelujah' you surprised us in church and each time you smiled it hurt. He missed it. The point and the promise. And when you ask for him in my soul I burn, because in your callow tone I hear you yearn… Excuse me. 'God do it now! Fill him with what he's missing. Soothe him where my kisses can't reach and perfect him in areas I'm not abreast to teach'. The letter is I. Will pray when I'm out of answers and you're full of questions. I. Love you more than words can rhyme. I. Vow you'll be an Amazing man because, You Are Mine! I call you my Sun because your arrival caused my spirit to shine. Yes. You are the greatest extension of God's love for me. He gave me you and because of how deep He dug for me. I was gone deep in sorrow. Not caring of the cares of tomorrow. I needed to see a branch of His love. I cry for your strength for I can't take credit. You have my beloved Granddaddy's spirit. Strong. Considerate. Mature and perfectly humorous. The letter is U. You embody the very ability to survive in the midst of confusion. You keep me. Stabilize that which once was shaky. I now know my purpose. Mother. Wow. Thank you both for choosing me…

by A Comeaux

Always Your Roll Dawg

Me and daddy do them highways dirty! Ridin' clean in the Cadi, stay fresh, stay flirty. He's 50 I'm 30 and no matter my life's ills, with him, nothing can hurt me! He's been my life's best friend and will be til I leave. He's the light behind my smile and the tear when I grieve. He's the lie he taught me to tell for the world to believe. I'm ok. Even when I'm not, it's ok because I'm made from a thoroughbred and a scholar. I can read my way into a paycheck or hustle up on my dollars. The best of both worlds but it's a curse indeed. Never thought from my first love I'd continually bleed. He left home too soon, then there was just me. I heard the cries he wasn't there to see. I was her party of 2 when there were supposed to be 3. But me and him, we understand each other. Beat to our drummer. Heartbreakers by nature, heat hotter than summer. But we're emotional and well spoken so we get them to see. Our way of living is the soooo the way to be! Free. To ride those highways at the whim of life's wind. All I ever wanted was for him to come home. No? Okay. Then as soon as I'm able I'll roam. I'll leave her too and denounce our home. Damn I tripped out! Never knew how kicking a door in would be the aftermath of when you slipped out. And it's different now. I get it. It'll never be what we all once were. And it's ok, I seek, today, my own family and my love will concur. Yes, I'm broken, searching my pieces. It's because I was lost without you and lack of love is my pain's thesis. But when life deals you a hand you can't play, I'm your roll dawg still to this day! When life or love threw blows, compass broken spirit and couldn't find our way, we were each others light to find the others way. Because, well, when you're good, I'm ok. When I smile, it's on your face. And no man, no woman could ever replace, this sacred space. And that's fine. You hold the dearest part of my heart and I have my place. Memories you gave me that have blessed my life. You gave me the 'game' to make me a better woman and eventual wife. You told me raw truth of what a man's to be. How to handle myself and demand how others treat me. Every time you left home, you came to where you were safe. In a sense you came home, always to my place. And I did the same, when life did me dirty and I lost in the game. When my love broke me, and confused my path, you were there to keep me on task. Right there with help before I could ask! I tear up when I think of the road trip we took Spring 2010. We hit highway, for ole times sake once again. All of us and we drove like never before. From Minnesota to Louisiana and all states between to explore. 'WHO DAT WHO DAT' soon as we walked through true Comeaux's door! Priceless. And then you bought all the girls diamonds from Texas, nickname me Ice Miss! Aunts and cousins and family embraced us like we were home. It was then I realized I no longer needed to roam. I'm your roll dawg and no matter where I am, we're always home. I love you because I am you and with that I know I'm never alone. First born carries your name because he needs a legacy to follow, not perfect, but genuine and for the weak you're a cold piece to swallow. Me? I'm your roll dawg and all you have to do is say the word. Gas up. Radio on blast and we're gone in our wind. My daddy. Your best friend…